Dubrovnik

THE BRADT CITY GUIDE

Piers Letcher

Bradt Travel Guides Ltd, UK
The Globe Pequot Press Inc, USA

First published 2005

Bradt Travel Guides Ltd, 19 High Street, Chalfont St Peter, Bucks SL9 9QE, England
Published in the USA by The Globe Pequot Press Inc, 246 Goose Lane, PO Box 480,
Guilford, Connecticut 06437-0480

Text copyright © 2005 Piers Letcher
Maps copyright © 2005 Bradt Travel Guides Ltd

A catalogue record for this book is available from the British Library

ISBN-10: 1 84162 109 9
ISBN-13: 978184162 109 8

Cover Dubrovnik rooftops (Laurence Mitchell)
Text photographs Piers Letcher (PL), Tricia Hayne (TH),
Maps Steve Munns
Illustrations Carole Vincer

Typeset from the author's disc by Wakewing
Printed and bound in Spain by Grafo SA, Bilbao

Author

Born and educated in the UK, Piers Letcher has lived in France for the past 20 years. As an independent writer and photographer he has published 15 books, more than a thousand newspaper and magazine articles and hundreds of photographs. From the mid-'90s he spent several years as a speechwriter at the United Nations in Geneva, before returning to his freelance career in 2002. He is the author of *Eccentric France* and *Croatia: The Bradt Travel Guide* and contributes irregularly to *The Guardian Unlimited*. *Dubrovnik* is his seventh guidebook.

FEEDBACK REQUEST

At Bradt Travel Guides we're well aware that guidebooks start to go out of date on the day they're published – and that you, our readers, are out there in the field, doing research of your own. You'll find out before us when a fine new family-run hotel opens or a favourite restaurant changes hands and goes downhill. So why not write to us and tell us about your experiences, for the next edition? We'll send you the Bradt Travel Guide of your choice and include you in the acknowledgments next time around if we use your feedback. So write to us – we'll look forward to hearing from you!

Piers Letcher – bradtcroatia@yahoo.co.uk

Contents

contents

Contents

Acknowledgements

First and sincerest thanks must go to Zrinka Jelavić at Adriatic Luxury Hotels, who did wonders in making difficult and busy research trips in 2004 a whole lot easier than they might have been. Special thanks, too, to Marc van Bloemen, who has quite the best place to stay in the old town (and to Bridget and Dominic Medley for putting me in touch with him), and to Kathy Ljubojević who was a mine of information. Thanks must also go to Niko Čučković, master glass designer, Niko Radić, for his sculpture of Sveti Vlaho, Niko Kobila, for his chauffeuring, Đeni Vokojević at the Grand Villa Argentina, Antun Maračić at the Museum of Modern Art, and Sanja Čimić and Wade Goddard at War Photo Limited. Iris Bear and her son Dan cheered up lunch one dull day, and my best wishes go to Helena Deranja and Igor Bulum (and hi to Sandra and Marko) from Atlas for their help on and off ferries. And thanks too, of course, to the staff at the Dubrovnik Tourist Board, who did their best to help me out and field my questions.

On Koločep I'd like to thank Marje Musladin, while on Lopud my sincerest gratitude to Vicko Radić of Elaphiti Travel who helped out in every conceivable way (and introduced me to Don Ivan Vlašić, who showed me round the museum and treasury). Thanks too, to Vicko's partner at Elaphiti Travel, Slobodan Varezić. On Šipan I'd like to thank Brian and Jane Foster for a great impromptu picnic, and Stanley Stjepović for taking me off the beaten track. On Mljet, my special thanks go to Zeljko Resetar at the Hotel Odisej.

For helping with the guide but also for being a great friend I'd like to thank Rajko Zorić (and his wife Ksenija and daughter Ema). For their feedback and input I'm grateful to Kris Dehamers and Michael Shaw, and as always I'd like to thank all the people at Bradt Travel Guides whose hard work make these books the best in their field. And of course, a heartfelt thank you to all the other people whose names I never caught, who offered help, hospitality and kindness along the way.

Finally, as always, I am indebted to Sarah Parkes (my sun and moon) for her kindness and thoughtfulness, her company and help in researching this book, and her generous spirit. Thanks too must go to Brice and Alec, who do a great deal, in the best possible sense, to distract me, and to my parents, who are more supportive than they probably realise.

Acknowledgements

DEDICATION

To Sarah Parkes – and to all the people who make Dubrovnik the extraordinary place it is.

Introduction

I've had a love affair with Croatia for more than 20 years, ever since I first inter-railed round Europe in 1982 and got stranded in Split for four days, waiting to meet someone who never showed up. It wasn't difficult to find my way from there to Dubrovnik, or to be entranced forever by the city once I got there.

It wasn't long before I was hammering at Hilary Bradt's door and clamouring to write about (what was then) Yugoslavia. That book came out in 1989, just in time to be washed away by the war – I spent 1991 glued to the television set, watching in horror as Dubrovnik was shelled, and had to wait a decade for my second chance to write about it. My guide to Croatia was published in 2003 (with a second edition in 2005), but between these covers I trust you'll find the most comprehensive, useful and up-to-date city guide to Dubrovnik.

DUBROVNIK AT A GLANCE

Location Right down at the southern end of Croatia's long coastline. Longitude 18°70 E, Latitude 42°28 N

Population 4,000 in the old town; 44,000 in greater Dubrovnik

Language Croatian

Religion Roman Catholic (85%); Muslim (5%); Orthodox Christian (4%)

Time CET (GMT +1 hour)

International telephone code +385 20 (local code 020 across the whole of southern Dalmatia)

Currency Kuna. €1 = 7.6 kuna, £1 = 10.8 kuna, US$1 = 6 kuna (December 2004)

Electricity 220v; two-pin plugs

Public holidays January 1; Easter Monday; May 1; Corpus Christi; June 22; June 25; August 5; August 15; October 8; November 1; December 25; December 26

Feast day February 3 (St Blaise)

Climate Mediterranean; 240 days/2,500 hours of sunshine

Contexts

INTRODUCTION TO THE CITY

Dubrovnik is an extraordinary place. Vast walls, up to 25m tall, come complete with fortresses, towers, crenellations and an ancient footpath along the entire 2km extent. The walls encircle an incredible stone-built red-roofed city, which juts out into the clearest, cleanest blue-green waters of the Adriatic. The streets are paved with time-polished pale marble, with the town's harmony owing as much to the 17th-century rebuilding programme following the Great Earthquake in 1667 as it does to Dubrovnik's remarkable history, stretching back well over a thousand years.

Of course Byron's 'Pearl of the Adriatic' is no secret, and in 2003 over 300,000 people stayed at least one night here. Even more came in for the day, on a record 582 cruise ships. Nevertheless the city copes admirably with the influxes, and you'll find a place full of cheerful cafés, bars and restaurants, wonderful architecture, intriguing museums, atmospheric churches and a world-famous Summer Festival. The entire old city is a UNESCO World Heritage Site.

As if that weren't enough, Dubrovnik is blessed with a kind climate. The minimum winter temperature rarely falls below 12°C, the sun shines reliably right through the summer, and there are plenty of beaches, with swimming popular from May to October. The city even has its own perfect forested island, Lokrum, just a few hundred metres offshore.

Dubrovnik in quotes

My trusty 1911 *Encyclopaedia Britannica* gets it right as usual, by fairly describing Dubrovnik as 'by far the most picturesque city on the Dalmatian coast' – though with it being pre-1918, they were still talking about Ragusa at the time. Far more famous, and certainly more quoted, is Lord Byron's remark about Dubrovnik being 'the Pearl of the Adriatic'. Almost equally over-used is the comment attributed to George Bernard Shaw, who was here in 1929 and came away telling people that 'those who seek paradise on earth should come to Dubrovnik'. After many hours of research, however, I've failed to find reliable sources for either quote. If you know the answers drop me a line and we'll happily include them in the next edition.

Altogether less enthusiastic was the ever-opinionated Rebecca West. On passing through in 1937, researching her magnum opus on the Balkans, *Black Lamb and Grey Falcon*, she said: 'I can't bear Dubrovnik. It reminds me of the worst of England.' Her husband, Henry Maxwell Andrews, couldn't agree. 'Dubrovnik is exquisite,' he riposted, 'perhaps the most exquisite town I have ever seen.' Later on – after visiting the cathedral treasury, in fact – he went on to add that he thought his spouse probably hated Dubrovnik simply 'because it poses so many questions that neither you nor anybody else can answer.'

What's in a name?

For most of its extensive history – right from the 7th century through to 1918, in fact – Dubrovnik was known as Ragusa. The name was changed to Dubrovnik (according to Rebecca West, at least) only because Ragusa sounded too Italian by half.

The truth, as usual, is somewhat more complicated. Dubrovnik was originally not one place but two, divided by what's now the main street, Stradun. On the seaward side, which was originally almost an island, was Ragusa, which was populated by people of Roman origin. On the landward side, populated by Slavs, was Dubrovnik. Given that the nobles all came (or claimed to come) from Roman stock, Ragusa was the name which stuck – until the city was incorporated into the newly founded Kingdom of Serbs, Croats and Slovenes after World War I.

The name Ragusa is thought to be a corruption of the Greek word *lausa*, meaning rock, while the name Dubrovnik comes from the Croatian word for oak woods, *dubrava* – which were once plentiful on the hills above the town before being cut down and used to build Dubrovnik's impressive fleet of ships. (A fleet of ships which gave us another word, incidentally – *argosy*, a version of the name Ragusa.)

St Blaise/Sveti Vlaho

Every Catholic town has its patron saint, but some are more venerated than others. Dubrovnik, with St Blaise (Sveti Vlaho, in Croatian), gives its patron saint the same sort of respect that Venice grants St Mark. You'll see statues of St Blaise above the town gates, in niches around the city, on the old state flag and coins of the republic, and even on the cannons.

The story goes that it was St Blaise (sometime in the late 10th century) who whispered in the ear of a local priest that Venetians supposedly in town on a courtesy visit were in fact up to no good, and had two fleets ready to attack, one hidden behind the island of Lokrum and the other over in the harbour at Gruž. Forewarned was forearmed, and the Venetians were sent packing.

In gratitude the city made St Blaise its patron, and so it has been since the year 972 – though it wasn't until 1026 that the city was able to buy St Blaise's head and various other relics from Byzantium. On February 3, Blaise's Day, his relics are paraded around Dubrovnik, and from 1190 onwards criminals and debtors who had been expelled from Ragusa could come back into town for the day.

Nothing is known for sure about St Blaise himself – though legend has it that he was a physician who went on to become the Bishop of Sebaste, in Armenia, back in the early 4th century. He lived in a cave (as you do) and sick animals would come spontaneously to him to be healed – though not of course bothering him if he was praying.

Agricola, the governor of Cappadocia at the time, came to Sebaste in about the year 316 for a spot of Christian-bashing, and sent out his huntsmen to capture wild animals for the next games at the arena (presumably destined also to feature Christians on the menu). What they found, to their surprise, was a load of unwell wild animals waiting outside Blaise's cave for him to finish his prayers.

Blaise was duly arrested and thrown into jail, where he did a good job of healing fellow-prisoners, including saving a child who was choking to death on a fish-bone

– which is how Blaise also got to be the patron saint of sore throats, and why even now people have their throats blessed on February 3.

This was all too much for Agricola, so he had Blaise thrown into a lake – but Blaise walked on water (literally) and his persecutors drowned trying to catch him. When he returned to shore, he was properly martyred – and remains one of the very few people ever thought to have been combed to death. Iron wool-combs were used to card his flesh, and then he was beheaded just for safety's sake.

He was duly rewarded by being designated one of the 'Fourteen Holy Helpers' and is the patron saint not just for throat ailments but also for a variety of professions, including those involved in the wool trade, builders, construction workers and vets.

HISTORY

Although some Roman, Illyrian and early Christian remains have been found in Dubrovnik, it was only at the beginning of the 7th century that the area was permanently settled. Survivors from the Roman colony at Salona (near Split), which had been taken over by avaricious Avars, teamed up with the remnants of the colony at Epidaurus (now Cavtat), which had been ravaged by Slavs, and settled on the rocky outcrop which is now the part of the old town south of Stradun. Doubtless scarred by their recent experiences, they started building fortifications right away – and kept on doing so until the 16th century. They called their town Ragusa, which first shows up in print in the year 667.

Slavs, meanwhile, settled on the lower slopes of Mount Srđ, across the marshy channel which would become Stradun. Over the centuries the populations mixed, the channel was filled in, and the city walls grew to encompass both parts of the settlement. But even today there's a clear distinction between the steep narrow streets leading uphill from Stradun to the north and the palaces, churches and open squares which characterise the rest of the city to the south. To their dying day (which we'll get to in a little while) Ragusan patricians insisted they could trace their lineage back to Roman rather than Slav ancestors.

Under the protection of Byzantium, Ragusa made steady progress and was one of the few Dalmatian settlements to resist a 15-month-long rampage by an army of Saracens in the 9th century. A hundred years later or so, in 992, Ragusa wasn't so lucky when the Macedonian ruler Tsar Samuel burned down the town – though his army had its comeuppance in 1014 when 14,000 of them had their eyes put out after losing a crucial battle against Byzantium.

Under Venice

After switching between Byzantium and Venice and back again, and even throwing in its lot with the Normans on a couple of occasions at the end of the 11th century, Ragusa finally recognised that Venice was top dog in the Adriatic in 1205, and remained under Venetian sovereignty until 1358. It nonetheless kept its own currency and continued to develop its own institutions and culture.

Ragusa was also becoming a trading state of increasing importance, capitalising on its fortunate position between north and south and east and west. By the early 13th century favourable trading agreements were in place with many of the Italian city states and far inland into the Balkans. Over the years it developed a strong seafaring tradition, with trade routes eventually established all the way to Spain, Portugal and England. Dubrovnik sailors were even on board Columbus's ships when they discovered the West Indies in 1492.

Back at home the early 14th century saw a number of important developments. After a huge fire destroyed most of the city in 1296, a new urban plan was developed. Dominicans and Franciscans were allowed inside the city walls for the first time, on condition that they defended the two main land gates at either end of Stradun – where you'll still find their respective monasteries and churches today. The Dominicans, confusingly, were called white friars here but black friars everywhere else. The Franciscans for their part made history in Dubrovnik by opening Europe's first pharmacy in 1317.

The city's first hospital was inaugurated in 1347, but was all too quickly followed in 1348 by a seriously nasty dose of the plague, which reduced the population by 8,000.

The Golden Age
Dubrovnik's Golden Age can fairly be said to begin when it finally escaped Venice's grasp by concluding the treaty of Višegrad with Ladislas the Great, the King of Hungary and Croatia, on June 25 1358. Under the treaty, Dubrovnik formally

became part of the Hungarian–Croatian kingdom, but in exchange for paying Hungary 500 ducats a year, and providing armed forces when called upon to do so, the republic was in fact allowed to do pretty much whatever it liked.

The first thing it liked to do, it seemed, was to frogmarch the Venetian rector, Marco Saranzo, off to his state galley, thereby kicking off the best part of 500 years of tension between the two republics – a situation only resolved when Napoleon dissolved *La Serenissima* in 1797.

In 1365, just seven years after sorting things out with Hungary, Dubrovnik signed a treaty with Sultan Murat I – again with a 500-ducat per year price tag – which allowed the republic free trading status across the whole of the occupied territories of the Ottoman Empire. By monopolising large chunks of the trade to and from the interior, Dubrovnik became hugely wealthy. At the end of the 15th century it had over seven million ducats in the state treasury – a great deal when you consider that at the time you could buy the town of Ston, along with its vital and lucrative salt manufactures, for just 120,000 ducats.

Dubrovnik had freedom, liberty and independence – but it was *Libertas* (the republic's long-standing motto) bought with gold. Nevertheless, gold was abundant. At its peak Dubrovnik – with a population of between 30,000 and 40,000 – had a fleet of over 300 ships, giving it the third-biggest cargo capacity in the world. And the ships were hugely profitable. It was reckoned that each only needed to make two voyages to cover the costs of building it – yet many of them lasted for decades.

With money came territory, and during the Golden Age Dubrovnik's lands stretched from the town of Neum to the north (now in Bosnia) all the way to Sutorina, on the Bay of Kotor, to the south (now in Montenegro), a distance of around 120km. It included the Elaphite Islands (Koločep, Lopud and Šipan), the islands of Mljet and Lastovo, and the Pelješac peninsula. For a heady three years in the early 15th century Dubrovnik even lorded it over the islands of Korčula, Hvar and Brač, but Venice was quick to reclaim sovereignty.

At the beginning of the 15th century the remaining wooden houses in the town were demolished and rebuilt in stone. This was not so much for aesthetic reasons as to prevent fires from spreading. With many potential enemies, Dubrovnik had large stockpiles of munitions, and they had an unfortunate habit of going off – the Rector's Palace was destroyed by fire and explosions twice within a generation, in 1435 and then again in 1463.

The 15th century also saw Dubrovnik flourishing as a haven of liberalism. It offered asylum to refugees, including Jews, at times when many other cities turned them away at the gate. In one instance, Dubrovnik enraged Sultan Murat II by taking in one of the Serb Princes after they'd been catastrophically defeated by the Turks at the battle of Kosovo Polje in 1389. But Dubrovnik responded: 'We men of Ragusa live only by our faith and according to that faith we would have sheltered you also, had you fled hither.'

In 1416 slavery was definitively abolished, over 400 years ahead of Britain (1833) and America (1863). Many slaves subsequently had their freedom bought for them

History

RAGUSA'S POLITICAL SYSTEM

Ragusa's political system was a variant on that of its rival Venice, though it was somewhat more subtle and complex. Of the three classes – nobles, commoners and workers – only the first exercised any power.

The main governing body was the Great Council, which consisted of all the male nobles over the age of 20; their main function was to elect the head of state, the rector, and supervise the Senate. The Senate comprised 45 nobles over the age of 40, though it had a purely consultative mandate. From the Senate, five men over the age of 50 were given a one-year term by the Great Council as *Proveditores*, keepers of the legal statutes and the constitution.

Executive power was wielded by the Minor Council, which consisted of 11 nobles appointed by the rector, with the youngest taking on the role of Foreign Minister. After the Great Earthquake of 1667 (see page 14), with fewer patricians to hand (and inhabitants to govern) the Minor Council was reduced to seven .

The rector had a term of office of just one month, during which he lived alone in the Rector's Palace, separated from his family and the rest of society. He was only allowed to leave the palace on state business or to attend church, and couldn't be re-elected within two years. In spite of all these restrictions he was merely a figurehead, wielding no power.

From 1205 to 1358 the rector was Venetian; from 1358 until the fall of the

Contexts

republic he was always Ragusan. The Hungarian king gave the rector the title of Arch Rector and the Order of the Golden Spur, but the Great Council wouldn't let him use either – though the Golden Spur did appear (somewhat mockingly) on a dead rector's coffin.

The political system was designed to concentrate power into the hands of a trusted few – in the 15th century there were only 33 noble families – but to avoid any one person or family being able to dominate. For centuries it worked remarkably effectively. The only time someone went for an individual power grab, early in the republic's history, he found himself without support from anyone but the workers, and was speedily forced to suicide. And although a small group of nobles did plot a coup in the 17th century – after being egged on by the Duke of Savoy – they were arrested before the fact at a masked ball and swiftly executed.

The class system was rigidly enforced. Inter-marriage between classes was forbidden and social relations between them strongly discouraged – though that doesn't seem to have been necessary, given the divisions even within classes. The nobles defined themselves as Salamancans or Sorbonnais, named after the respective Spanish and French universities, with the former sympathetic to Spanish Absolutism and the latter with a liberal francophile outlook. Apparently hostility was such that members of the two factions couldn't even bring themselves to greet one another in the street.

MARIN GETALDIĆ – FRIEND OF GALILEO, PRECURSOR OF NEWTON

Marin Getaldić (Marino Ghetaldi in Italian) was born into a noble Ragusan family in 1568, and showed early promise as a natural philosopher. He went on to study in Rome, Padua (where he met and befriended Galileo Galilei), Antwerp and Paris (where he was greatly influenced by the noted French mathematician François Viète), before spending two years in England. He was offered the prestigious chair of mathematics at Louvain University in Belgium but turned it down, preferring to return home to Ragusa.

Getaldić set up a laboratory in a cave where he performed a prodigious range of physical and mathematical experiments, and his work in optics, geometry and algebra was the precursor to Newton's. He usefully worked out the relative weight of a number of elements including gold, silver, copper, lead and mercury, and perhaps less usefully that of wine, honey, oil and wax.

by Ragusan nobles. A public health service was in place as early as 1432, while the principle of education for all was established three years later, along with one of Europe's first orphanages and a free retirement home for the poor and elderly (it's still running, but no longer free).

His most interesting work, however, was on a formidable parabolic mirror, 66cm in diameter (which can be found in the Maritime Museum in Greenwich, if you're interested). This was powerful enough to melt lead and silver at a distance, and was thought by the natives to be a danger to local shipping. The cave where he worked became known as 'Bête's Cave' (the cave of the beast) after Getaldić's rather unfortunate nickname.

Unlucky nickname or not, Getaldić became a prominent figure in local politics – as a noble he was by default a member of the Great Council but he also served on the Minor Council, and was the Ragusan envoy to Constantinople in 1606. He also found time to publish a number of significant works including *Promotus Archimedus* (1603) and *Variorum problematum colletio* (1607), a handy pamphlet detailing the solutions to 42 tricky geometrical problems.

He died in Ragusa in 1626. His magnum opus, *De resolutione et compositionem mathematica* was published four years later.

The republic's wealth was also put to good use in a major building programme. The city walls were reinforced and defensive fortresses and towers constructed along their length. Onofrio della Cava, a bright engineer and architect from Naples, spent the six years to 1444 putting in place a sophisticated water supply (including an 8km aqueduct) which still works today and powers the two Onofrio fountains on Stradun. In 1468 Stradun itself was repaved with marble, and in 1516 work began on the Customs House (formerly called the Divona and now known as the Sponza Palace).

Unfortunately an earthquake destroyed most of the city in 1520, and the plague returned in force in 1528, leaving 20,000 dead.

By the end of the 1520s, the Turks had pretty much defeated Hungary, and Dubrovnik was quick to change its allegiance from the Hungarian king to the Turkish sultan – now agreeing to pay an annual tribute of 12,500 ducats to keep the peace. The money was taken to the Sublime Porte every two years by envoys who then had to spend the next two years waiting there as effective hostages until they were relieved by the next cash-laden delegation.

In 1588 Dubrovnik joined the Spanish in their 'Invincible Armada' and lost a dozen of its finest ships. As a result, trade with Britain was interrupted for the best part of two centuries. The battle neatly marks the beginning of the long, slow, decline of the republic. New trade routes across the Atlantic made Britain, Spain and Portugal into wealthy nations, and Mediterranean shipping was never to regain its former importance.

The Great Earthquake

Real disaster didn't strike until 08.00 on April 6 1667, the Saturday before Easter, when a massive earthquake destroyed Dubrovnik. More than 5,000 people – including the rector, the entire Minor Council and more than half the Great Council

– were killed. Four times the harbour emptied itself of water and returned, dashing ships to pieces and drowning survivors under the rubble. A raging fire broke out and looters pillaged the city.

Only the Sponza Palace, the two monasteries, the bottom half of the Rector's Palace and the Revelin fortress were left standing. The last was the saving of the city, as the treasury was hastily moved there out of harm's way. The remaining nobles cleared the city of looters (presumably at gunpoint), and diplomatically persuaded the Turks and Venetians – who were waiting opportunistically nearby – that Dubrovnik didn't actually need their help.

It was all too tempting for the sultan, however, who asked for a vast ransom to be paid if Dubrovnik wanted its freedom to continue as before. A delegation was sent in 1673 to the Porte to … well, 'talk turkey' with the Turks. Among the party were Nikola Bono, who had persuaded the Venetians to leave the devastated city in 1667, and Marojica Koboga, who had done the same with the Turks. After months of wrangling they were thrown into a plague-stricken prison, where (in the rather graphic words of Rebecca West) 'they lay for years, sometimes smuggling home dispatches written in their excrement on packing paper.'

Nikola Bono was to die in prison, but after the Turks were defeated at Vienna in 1683, Koboga came home to a hero's welcome. Dubrovnik had got away without paying the ransom, and was still free. It consolidated its position in 1699 by letting the Turks have chunks of land at either end of its territories – which is why today Neum is in Bosnia not Croatia, and Sutorina is in Montenegro. This

RUĐER BOŠKOVIĆ – MATHEMATICAL GENIUS AND LATIN POET

Pictures of Ruđer Bošković (Ruggero Boscovich in Italian) – a brilliant mathematician and physicist born in Ragusa in 1711 – show a man with a slightly pudgy face and the permanent, slightly exasperated look of the over-intelligent.

He was educated in Ragusa by the Jesuits and then went on at the age of 14 to study at the Jesuit *Collegium Romanum* in Rome – so successfully that he was appointed professor of mathematics and physics there at the tender age of 29. As one of Europe's brightest scientists, Bošković was a member of London's Royal Society and wrote around 70 papers on astronomy, gravitation, meteorology, optics and trigonometry. His most famous work is *A Theory of Natural Philosophy* – or *Philosophiae naturalis theoria redacta ad unicam legem*

meant that potential attacks from Venice could now only come from the sea and not overland.

Although Dubrovnik would never regain its former glories, the massive programme of rebuilding which went on through the early 18th century was to deliver the harmonious city you see today. Height restrictions were placed on all buildings, for fear of another earthquake, and most of the houses were built to the *virium in Natura existentium,* as it's more correctly known.

From the late 1750s he travelled widely in Europe before taking up a post as the professor of mathematics at Pavia in 1764. As the director of the Brera Observatory he led an expedition in 1769 to observe the transit of Venus across the face of the sun (for those of you who missed it in 2004 your last chance this lifetime will be 2012 – unless you plan on living until the year 2117). Unfortunately he missed the event, as his ship was caught in a storm – and the next transit wasn't going to happen until 1874.

By 1770 he was working in Milan, before moving on to Venice and then Paris, but he always spared a thought for Ragusa, and lamented not having the time to visit. Bošković was also something of a Latin poet and was capable of describing his complex astronomical ideas in elegant metered verse. He died in Milan in 1787.

same design, with a shop on the ground floor and living quarters above. The entrance door and window were combined in the distinctive *'na koljeno'* single-arched frame, to provide a counter over which goods could be served to customers (though these days they've mostly been permanently glazed in). By 1713 the new baroque cathedral was open for business, followed in 1717 by St Blaise's Church next door, and in 1725 by the Jesuit church just up the hill.

History

Things started to look up for the republic, and by the end of the 18th century it had regained a considerable amount of its wealth and standing, and even boasted some 80 consulates in various cities across the continent.

Unfortunately, though, Napoleon was on the horizon.

The Fall

Things must have looked pretty shaky for Dubrovnik in 1797, when Napoleon took over Venice and put an end to *La Serenissima*'s 1,100-year history, but for nearly a decade Dubrovnik managed to survive as the only neutral state in the Mediterranean. But on May 26 1806 – as the only way to break a month-long siege by Russian and Montenegrin forces – the republic allowed a French garrison led by General Jacques Alexandre de Lauriston to enter the town. (Even now, clocks in the city's museums are often set to 17.45, the hour at which the troops entered the city.)

It's sometimes said that Lauriston only asked for safe passage on his way to take the Bay of Kotor, but either way – needless to say – once installed the French didn't leave. On January 31 1808 the republic was finally abolished and the following year was absorbed into the newly created French 'Illyrian Provinces', which stretched all the way up the Adriatic coast to Trieste. One of Napoleon's favourite generals, Auguste Marmont, now promoted to Marshal, became the region's governor, holding the titles of both Duc de Raguse and Duc de Spalato (Split).

The French did a pretty good job in the Illyrian Provinces, building roads (including the road from Pile to Gruž, still in use today), improving healthcare and education and making life generally more equitable for most people, under the Napoleonic code. They encouraged the culture of the south Slavs and the first Croatian-language newspapers saw publication.

The occupiers were nonetheless greatly resented, and in 1813, at the behest of the British and Austrians, Dubrovnik revolted, and was briefly recognised as an independent state again (by the British, anyway). It was all very short-lived. As soon as Napoleon had been defeated at Leipzig on October 16, Austria sent troops south and took control of Dubrovnik on January 28 1814. It was officially annexed into Austria (later the Austro-Hungarian Empire) the following year.

Dubrovnik's noble families, in a terminal huff, took a vow of celibacy and swiftly died out.

Into the 20th century

Dubrovnik remained annexed to the Austro-Hungarian Empire until the end of World War I, when it became part of the newly created Kingdom of Serbs, Croats and Slovenes, under the Crown of King Petar I from the dynastic Karađorđevic family.

Petar was succeeded on his death, three years later, by his son, King Aleksandar I, who 'reluctantly' suspended parliament in 1929 after a Croatian firebrand called Stjepan Radić was fatally shot in Belgrade's parliamentary chamber by a Montenegrin deputy. Aleksandar established a dictatorship, but at least put diplomats and letter writers across the continent out of their misery by changing

history

the country's name to the more manageable Yugoslavia – the country of the South Slavs.

In 1934 Aleksandar was assassinated in Marseille, in a plot sponsored by the Ustaše, a fascist party founded five years earlier by Ante Pavelić, and left the ill-equipped Prince Petar to run the country – aged only 11. Yugoslavia limped on, even managing to remain neutral for the first year and a half of World War II, but quickly fell when Germany attacked in April 1941.

Once Yugoslavia had thrown in the towel, the Ustaše declared the Independent State of Croatia (*Nezavisna Država Hrvatska*, NDH), which included Dubrovnik, with Ivo Rojnica as its prefect. One of the first things he did, on June 25 1941, was to give the order that Serbs and Jews could neither work nor be on the streets between 19.00 and 07.00.

(Rojnica escaped to Argentina after the war, but remains a controversial figure. The first Croatian president, Franjo Tuđman, presented him with a medal and asked him to be Croatia's Ambassador to Argentina in 1992 – even after Rojnica had reportedly said: 'Everything I did in 1941 I would do again.' Tuđman backed down under international pressure, but Rojnica continues to make the news. In July 2003, the Simon Wiesenthal Centre, which hunts down Nazi war criminals, urged Stipe Mesić, Croatia's president, to press on with investigations against Rojnica.)

The NDH controlled Dubrovnik until September 1943, when Italy capitulated and the Germans took over. Thirteen months later the city was liberated by the

Partisans, the army of the Communist Party, led by Josip Broz 'Tito'. One of the first things the Partisans did was to arrest Dubrovnik's 44 leading intellectuals – including a number of priests – and execute them without trial on the island of Daksa, which sits just a few hundred metres from the port of Gruž. Dubrovnik rejoined Yugoslavia in 1945.

After World War II

Post-war elections not surprisingly gave the communists 90% of the vote – with separate ballot boxes provided for those who cared to vote against them. That gave the government the freedom to set up on the lines adopted by Stalinist Russia, and to embark on a disastrous experiment with collectivisation.

Fortunately Yugoslavia was saved by the launch of mass tourism in the 1960s, and did remarkably well until Tito's death in 1980. Unfortunately, Tito had left his country with a weak succession. Each of the republics would, in theory, get a year as head man, but without Tito's personal charisma and unifying strength it was never going to work well. It wasn't long before the old problems of nationalism, unfair distribution of wealth between the republics, and corruption in government resurfaced.

On to this scene arrived Slobodan Milošević, who rapidly gained popularity in Serbia after defending Serb protestors against mostly ethnic Albanian police in Kosovo in 1987. Two years later, on June 28 1989 (the 700th anniversary of the defeat at Kosovo Polje), Milošević addressed a million Serbs at the site of the battle and was elected President of Serbia in the autumn.

It was the beginning of the end for a united Yugoslavia. Milošević's bluster about an ethnically pure Greater Serbia was never going to sit well with Croats – or indeed Slovenes, Bosnians, Macedonians and Kosovars.

War – and Croatian independence

The 1989 collapse of the Soviet Union and the fall of communist governments across Europe encouraged several Yugoslav republics, led by Slovenia and Croatia, to try and change the political structure of Yugoslavia.

In 1990, led by former army general and dissident (some would prefer revisionist) historian Franjo Tuđman, the Croatian Democratic Union (HDZ), won elections. Once in power, the HDZ pushed parliament to drop the word 'Socialist' from the Croatian republic's name, and the red star was quietly removed from public signs.

The HDZ also put Croatia's 600,000 Serbs on the defensive by changing their status from 'constituent nation' in Croatia to 'national minority', and many Serbs in government lost their jobs. The HDZ didn't improve matters by making itself an easy target for Serb propaganda – party members playing straight into Serb hands by attempting to rehabilitate the Ustaše.

During the summer of 1990, encouraged by Belgrade into fearing real danger, Croatia's Serbs (armed by the Yugoslav People's Army, the JNA) declared an autonomous region around Knin, 100km northwest of Split. Croatian police helicopters, sent in to sort out the trouble, were soon scuttled by Yugoslav air force

MiGs. Tension continued to mount until March 1991, when Knin paramilitaries took control of the Plitvice lakes, resulting in the first casualties of the conflict.

Slovenia, meanwhile, had unilaterally decided it would declare independence on June 25 1991, so Croatia declared independence on the same day. Milošević sent tanks into Ljubljana, Slovenia's capital, and to the Italian and Austrian borders. The world sat up and took notice, and the EU introduced sanctions; within a week the war in Slovenia was over, and within a month the JNA had left the country – though it only retreated as far as Croatia, and later distributed many weapons to the local Serb population.

Croatia, with a significant Serb minority, wasn't as fortunate. As soon as it proclaimed independence, the Serbs countered by proclaiming the independent state of Republika Srpska Krajina (RSK) within Croatia, declaring loyalty to Belgrade and Milošević (the commander of the army), and choosing Knin as its capital.

In six months at the end of 1991 – with the help of the JNA, and heavy fighting, bombardments and air-strikes – the Serbs ethnically 'cleansed' nearly a third of Croatia, re-awakening memories of the brutality of the 1940s. Thousands of Croats were forced to leave their homes and many were killed by the JNA or loosely associated paramilitary forces. The tourist trade – one of Croatia's main sources of foreign earnings – came to a complete halt.

Dubrovnik was not spared. Indeed, despite the old town having been demilitarised by the JNA in the 1970s, precisely to avoid potential damage to one of the country's most important pieces of heritage, Dubrovnik became a tragic

THE SIEGE OF DUBROVNIK

In October 1991, with the war in full flow, the Yugoslav army laid siege to Dubrovnik, shutting off the water and electricity supplies, and raining shells down into the heart of the old town from air, land and sea.

The quick capitulation the Serbs expected never happened, mainly because of determined resistance, but at least in part because Onofrio's fountains – supplied by 15th-century plumbing – continued to function throughout the siege. Nevertheless, for three months there was no water for anything other than drinking, and no electricity or telephone service at all.

More than 100 civilians lost their lives in Dubrovnik, either when their houses were bombed or by snipers up in the hills, looking straight down Stradun – people simply didn't believe they were going to be shot in the sunny streets of Dubrovnik's old town. On one day alone (December 6 1991) the Serbs shelled the city from 05.00 to 16.10 with only a 15-minute break. In all the siege lasted from October 1991 to August 1992, though a ceasefire of sorts was in force at the beginning of 1992.

The material damage caused was enormous, with 70% of the old town's 800 houses sustaining direct hits, and more than 50 shells landing on Stradun alone. Many churches and monuments were targeted in spite of being clearly marked with UNESCO flags.

Dubrovnik's newly refurbished airport was completely destroyed, with the brand-new equipment being looted and taken back to Montenegro and on to Belgrade. Many people moved out, and not all have moved back – the old town's population, at 4,000, is still around 20% less than it was in 1990.

The damage sustained to Dubrovnik's reputation as a holiday destination was incomparably worse, and it took a full decade to bring back just half the visitors.

Yet Dubrovnik has made a truly heroic recovery from the war. Today, beyond a few pockmarked buildings, and acres of new tiles on the roofs, you'd never know there had been a terrible siege just a decade ago. (Ironically, some of the old tiles pulled off roofs during renovations were sent to villages further north to repair war damage there – only to be caught in the 1996 earthquake which destroyed much of Slano and Ston, at the base of the Pelješac peninsula.)

The only real reminder that the war happened at all – beyond the psychological scars – are the multi-lingual signs at each entrance to the old town, showing the 'City Map of Damages caused by the aggression on Dubrovnik by the Yugoslav Army, Serbs and Montenegrins, 1991–1992'.

Some justice has been done – in March 2004 a retired Yugoslav navy admiral, Miodrag Jokic, was sentenced to seven years in prison at The Hague for his part in shelling Dubrovnik.

victim of the conflict, suffering one of the toughest sieges of the war. The worst was over by the autumn of 1992, but it wasn't until 1996 that a peace treaty was signed between Croatia and Yugoslavia.

Key dates in the history of Ragusa/Dubrovnik

Early 7th century	Founding of Ragusa
667	First mention of the name Ragusium
972	St Blaise (Sveti Vlaho) chosen as patron saint
1026	Ragusa buys relics of St Blaise from Byzantium
11th century	The marshy land between Roman Ragusa and Slavic Dubrovnik is filled in
1272	The republic's statutes are codified in eight volumes
1296	A huge fire devastates the town
1317	Europe's first pharmacy opens
1348	8,000 die of the plague
1358	Ragusa officially becomes part of the Kingdom of Hungary and Croatia
1365	Treaty with Sultan Murat I
1416	Slavery abolished
1468	Stradun (Placa) repaved with marble
1520	An earthquake destroys much of the city
1528	The plague leaves 20,000 dead

1529	The Turks conquer Hungary; Ragusa transfers loyalty (and gold) to Turkey
1588	Ragusa joins the Spanish and their 'Invincible Armada'; it loses 12 ships
1667	The Great Earthquake destroys the city, kills the rector, most nobles and more than half the population
1806	Napoleon's troops arrive in town
1808	Dissolution of the republic
1815	Ragusa is annexed by Austria
1918	Dubrovnik becomes part of the Kingdom of Serbs, Croats and Slovenes (from 1929, Yugoslavia)
1941	Dubrovnik becomes part of the fascist NDH
1943	German troops take over after the fall of Italy
1944	City liberated by Tito's Partisans
1945	Dubrovnik again becomes part of Yugoslavia
1991–1992	The siege of Dubrovnik by Serb and Montenegrin forces
1992	Croatia receives formal recognition of nationhood from the international community

POLITICS

Independence brought Croatia a new constitution and a new political system which – as the Ministry of Foreign Affairs says on its website (www.mvp.hr) – is now 'democratic and based on a respect for human rights, law, national equality, social justice and multiple political parties'. The last part is certainly true, with a bewildering array of three- and four-letter acronyms to deal with. The really important one to remember is the HDZ, the nationalist Croatian Democratic Union, which was founded by the new nation's first president, Franjo Tuđman.

After Tuđman's death in 1999, the HDZ was trounced in parliamentary elections, and Stipe Mesić was elected president in 2000. In the most recent parliamentary elections, held at the end of 2003, the HDZ saw a return to form, winning 66 of the 151 seats available in the Sabor (parliament), and able to form a government via an informal coalition with other smaller parties. Both the president and the prime minister, Ivo Sanader, are keen to join NATO and the EU – although hopes that this might happen in 2006 for NATO and 2007 for the EU may be overly optimistic.

In Dubrovnik, support for the HDZ is strong, but there are the usual political wranglings you'd expect in any town, with gossip concerning corruption in local government and a certain amount of hand-wringing about how best to manage the city's principal source of revenue, tourism. Meanwhile there's also a pervasive level of mistrust of central government, which can be pinned down at least in part to Dubrovnik being as far away from the capital, Zagreb, as you can get within Croatia.

ECONOMY

Croatia is still paying the price of a legacy of communist mismanagement of the economy, as well as its more recent war, which left infrastructure damaged and

WESTERN TIES

Most businessmen dressing for work in the morning don't spare a thought for Croatia – which is a pity, as the ubiquitous neck-tie they put on not just originated there but is named after the country.

The origins of one of fashion's most durable accessories date back to the Thirty Years War in Europe, from 1618 to 1648. The story goes that Croatian mercenaries of the period wore a colourful silk scarf tied around the neck. Some of their number were stationed in Paris, and were presented to the court (whether that of Louis XIII, who died in 1643, or Louis XIV, who succeeded him, is debatable), triggering off a copycat craze for *cravates* – the word coming from dressing *à la Croat* (or *Hrvat*, in Croatian).

During the dandyish reign of Louis XIV, the wearing of *cravates* by Frenchmen became widespread, and the new fashion soon spread right across Europe – indeed the French word '*cravate*' exists in one form or another in almost every European language, from '*gravata*' in Greek to '*krawatte*' in German. Today, businessmen and politicians worldwide consider the tie as a basic part of their wardrobe – though for the most part they probably aren't wearing the enormously expensive long, floppy silk scarves favoured by Croatian soldiers, but the rather more sober ties which first appeared in England at the end of the 19th century.

large numbers of people displaced. Progress towards economic reform has been hampered by coalition politics and resistance on the street, mainly from trade unions, but the government is now keen to achieve EU membership, and the economy is looking in better shape than it has for years.

Inflation dropped to just 2.1% in 2003, and GDP, at close to US$40 billion (at purchasing power parity, PPP) grew by 4.3% from 2002 to 2003. Nonetheless, Croatian GDP per capita, at around US$8,800, is still under half that in Spain and around a third of that in the UK. Average gross salary in April 2004 had risen to 5,962 kuna per month (around €800), but unemployment, at 18.6%, was still stubbornly high.

Vital to the economy – especially along the coast – is tourism. In the year 2000 revenue from tourism finally exceeded the 1990 figures for the first time, and in 2003 was worth something like US$8 billion to Croatia's economy. The government expects this figure to reach US$20 billion within ten years.

TOURISM

Back in 1990, over 850,000 tourists spent a total of 5.4 million nights in Dubrovnik County. A year later the old town was besieged by Serbian forces, and tourism came to a spectacular and total halt. With Dubrovnik now restored to its former glories, more people are coming back every year, with an increase in 2003 alone of nearly 30% in foreign visitor numbers.

Nevertheless, while tourist nights in Croatia as a whole now exceed their 1990 levels, those in Dubrovnik were still a third down in 2003, with 3.7 million tourist nights being spent in the county (which includes the surrounding coast as far as the Pelješac peninsula and the island of Korčula). Dubrovnik itself saw just over 300,000 visitors spend 1.3 million nights in the city in 2003.

On top of that are the cruise ships, which mostly come in for the day. Numbers here are booming, with 582 ships visiting in 2003, up from just 307 a year earlier, and bringing in over 420,000 people – against 226,000 a year earlier.

The vast majority of visitors (over 85%) to Croatia are foreigners from the north in search of sea and sunshine. The most numerous among them in 2003 were Germans (1.5 million) and Italians (1.2 million), with the UK some way down the list, with 150,000 – though that's nearly half as many again as came in 2001.

It would be pointless to pretend the huge numbers of visitors don't have a huge impact on Dubrovnik. While the city and its people have become rich from tourist revenues, the single-minded focus on tourism has left its mark, and you'll notice few public facilities – especially in the old town – for the dwindling local population. There are fewer and fewer young people, especially. Back in the 1960s, there were half a dozen classes of 30 children each at the old town's school; by 2004 there were just two classes of 18 pupils each.

PEOPLE

In spite of the large displacement of people – both Serbs and Croats – during the war of the 1990s, Croatia's total population has remained fairly stable (at around 4.4 million) over the past 20 years. Dubrovnik, however, has seen its population steadily decline, from 54,000 in 1961 to 50,000 in 1991 and 44,000 in 2001. The old town, which had a population of over 5,000 in 1991, is home to barely 4,000 people today.

Ethnic demographics have also changed. In the 1991 census around three-quarters of people considered themselves Croats, while 12.2% said they were Serbs. A decade later, the 2001 census showed that almost 90% of people thought of themselves as Croats, while Serbs only accounted for 3.3% of the population. There are a number of reasons for the decline in Serb numbers, including the introduction of a new category, 'ethnically uncommitted' (which attracted 2% of the population in 2001), changes in the census methodology, and of course the exodus of Serbs from Croatia after the war.

However they describe themselves, most people in Dubrovnik are warm, hospitable and generous – although they have a reputation in other parts of Croatia for being somewhat 'special' (there's a certain amount of jealousy about Dubrovnik being such a nice place to live, too). When it's really busy you may find a certain brusqueness and reserve from waiting staff, but you'll find on the whole that people will treat you right if you treat them right.

RELIGION

In the 2001 census, some 87.8% of the Croatian population labelled themselves as Roman Catholics (up from three-quarters in 1991). With Catholicism long having been tied to Croatian national identity, it's as much a statement against Tito's brand of socialism or Serbia's Orthodox Church as it is a credo in itself. As a result, church attendance was hugely popular in the first years of Croatian independence, though has tailed off somewhat in recent years. Dubrovnik – always more secular than the rest of the country – registered 84.6% of the population Catholic in the 2001 census, with 5.3% Muslim, 3.9% Orthodox, 2.5% agnostic, 1.9% unbelievers and 0.01% Jewish.

The Church plays an important part in day-to-day life in Dubrovnik, and you'll often find people worshipping privately outside of church service times, or just popping in for a quick dab at the holy water; either way you should respect their quiet and privacy. Clothing restrictions in Dubrovnik are a bit more flexible than in some parts of the country, but you should nonetheless think twice about visiting religious buildings in beachwear.

Smaller churches are often closed outside the periods immediately before and after mass.

CULTURE AND FESTIVALS

While Dubrovnik is world-famous for its architectural heritage, there are few if any local artists, writers or composers well known outside Croatia. Partly that's because Ragusa countenanced no art other than literature until the republic fell (notwithstanding a brief foray into painting in the early 16th century, soon put paid to by the plague of 1528). As a result, Dubrovnik can boast two of Croatia's most famous writers, Marin Držić and Ivan Gundulić as natives, but it wasn't until 1869 that the city's first theatre was opened.

Today, the big cultural draw is Dubrovnik's Summer Festival, which runs for six weeks or so every year from July 10 to August 25. Every space that can be used for a concert or a theatrical performance is pressed into service as a temporary stage, and it's a great – if crowded – time to be in town (see page 130 for more details).

Thirty years ago you'd also see – and hear – plenty of Croatia's abundant folk music; Tito's communist government was unusual in encouraging people to retain their folk traditions. These days, however, it tends to be on show only for sporadic performances during the summer in Dubrovnik itself, though there are occasional shows put on at the bigger hotels too. But if you want the authentic, traditional, folk experience, Dubrovnik's not the best place to be – you're far better off heading up into Slavonia, in eastern Croatia.

That said, the Lindo dance troupe, which is based in Dubrovnik, does put on excellent shows. And some of the best traditional music I've ever been party to was at a wedding in Cavtat, just down the coast – so keep your ears pinned back, especially on Saturdays.

You'll also find a lot going on around religious festivals and holidays, with processions, masses and music aplenty. The calendar kicks off on February 3, St Blaise's feast day, and is followed up shortly with Easter and Corpus Christi, after which there's a long gap until All Saints' Day and then Christmas – which is much as you'd expect, though a big fish rather than a turkey takes pride of place at the main celebration, on Christmas Eve.

PUBLIC HOLIDAYS

Croatia has the usual European mix of religious and secular public holidays. Banks and most shops will close on these days:

January 1	New Year's Day
Easter Sunday and Easter Monday	Easter falls on Sunday March 27 in 2005, Sunday April 16 in 2006 and Sunday April 8 in 2007
May 1	Labour Day
Corpus Christi	60 days after Easter Sunday, and taken seriously in Croatia, with processions and lots of first communions (May 26 in 2005, June 15 in 2006 and June 7 in 2007)
June 22	Day of Antifascist Struggle
June 25	Statehood Day
August 5	Homeland Thanksgiving Day
August 15	Assumption of the Virgin Mary
October 8	Independence Day
November 1	All Saints' Day
December 25 and 26	Christmas holidays

GEOGRAPHY AND CLIMATE
Geography

Dubrovnik is situated right at the southern end of Croatia – the border with Montenegro is only 40km southeast, while just 5km over the mountains behind the city is Bosnia & Herzegovina (indeed Dubrovnik is technically cut off from the rest of Croatia by Bosnia's access to the sea, at Neum, 50km northwest).

Right next to the old town is the island of Lokrum, just a few hundred metres offshore, while stretched in a string northwest of town are the Elaphite islands, of which only three, Koločep, Lopud and Šipan, are inhabited. Even further offshore is the near-perfect island of Mljet, the western half of which is a national park. Due north of Mljet the rugged, wine-growing Pelješac peninsula stretches out into the Adriatic; it joins the mainland at Ston, formerly famous for its salt-pans but today the producer of Croatia's best oysters and mussels.

Climate

Dubrovnik has a great climate, with daily temperatures rarely falling below 12°C in winter or rising above 30°C in summer. Average highs stay above 16°C from March through to the end of November, while average lows range from 6.4°C in February to 21.7°C in August. There's oodles of sunshine – indeed, with an average of over 2,500 hours a year and 240 sunny days it's one of the sunniest places in Europe, so you'll find plenty of alfresco drinking and dining opportunities, even in winter.

That said, Dubrovnik does get more rain than you might expect, with an average of around 1,000mm a year – exactly midway between London's 600mm and Scotland's 1,400mm, but it does rain harder and faster here. Dubrovnik has 110 rainy days to London's 145, and most of those are in winter – typically there are only 21 rainy days between the beginning of June and the end of September, half as many as you might expect in a London summer.

NATURAL HISTORY AND CONSERVATION

The Dalmatian coast round Dubrovnik benefits from some of the cleanest waters in the Mediterranean. A happy accident of geography means that the water circulates anticlockwise around the Adriatic, bringing fresh, clean sea-water in along the Albanian coast to Dubrovnik. Sea currents then take the water all the way up the coast to Trieste and Venice (where it acts as an unsophisticated sewage system) before collecting everything that comes out of the Po Delta. It then flushes down the Italian coast and back out into the Mediterranean at Italy's heel – which is why the sea in Rimini and Ancona is muddy, but the waters in Dubrovnik are crystal-clear.

The coast hasn't been too over-developed, either. During Tito's days, Yugoslavia embarked on a progressive programme of tourist development, and although there are some pretty unattractive hotel complexes dating from that era, these were mostly (happily) kept out of the way of the main attractions.

Natural history

Few people come to Dubrovnik with natural history in mind, and from the point of view of fauna you're likely to see little more here than lizards, seagulls and whatever fish of the day happens to be served up on your lunch plate. You might also be

Aleppo pine

unimpressed with the flora in the old town, which is pretty much limited to a few houseplants, geraniums and oleanders in the narrow streets leading uphill off Stradun.

Outside the old town, however – and especially on the islands – there's a wide range of animal and plant life, ranging from several species of butterfly you won't find in Britain and Mljet's famous mongooses to a wealth of aromatic herbs, citrus fruits and abundant bougainvillea.

If you venture up the coast to Trsteno (see page 211) you can visit a wonderful arboretum from the early 16th century, complete with exotic plants, palms and giant plane trees. Further northwest still is the extraordinary Neretva Delta (see page 214), one of the Adriatic's most important waterfowl reserves, featuring swampy salt marshes, lagoons, reeds and meadows.

Environmental issues

The biggest environmental impact to affect Dubrovnik and the surrounding area in recent times was of course the serious destruction of infrastructure, heritage and natural resources caused by the war of the early 1990s. In spite of the quick repairs to the old town, it will take some time before all the damage is fixed (a couple of the big hotels, for example are still just burned-out concrete shells), and longer still before the countryside is fully restored to its natural state. Up in the hills marking the border with Bosnia there are still mines and unexploded ordnance to be found (though you won't be in any danger of straying into zones where this is the case; anything dangerous is fenced off and well marked).

Fire is another environmental hazard – a landscape which quickly absorbs what little water there is and a hot dry summer are a recipe for accidental combustion. The starting of any kind of fire in summer is strongly discouraged, and indeed strictly forbidden in the national parks. If you can't resist barbecuing, do so carefully, and be sure you have what it takes to put the flames out if things get out of control.

The area is also exposed to one other environmental risk: earthquakes. A major and active fault network runs through Italy and the Balkans, and it was an earthquake in 1667 that levelled most of Dubrovnik's public buildings (see page 14). The most recent serious earthquake occurred in 1996, with its epicentre in the area of Slano and Ston, 50km up the coast from Dubrovnik. Ston – now famous for its excellent oysters – was almost completely destroyed. Although there were fortunately no fatalities, around 2,000 people in the area lost their homes.

DUBROVNIK

Elaphite Islands, Mljet,
Korčula, Split, Zadar, Rijeka

Dubrovnik, Bari

Ferry

Beach

Beach

Beach

Nuncijata

BABIN KUK

GRUŽ

N

Bradt

0 _____ 1km
0 _____ ½mile

Beach

Beach

Beach

Srđ
412m

Beach

LAPAD

145m

192m

Bus station

DRŽAVANA CESTA

Airport 20km

Naturist beach

Hospital

BONINOVO

Taxis/Buses

PLOČE

Beaches

PILE

Beaches

Lovrijenac
Fortress

**OLD
TOWN**

Beach

Ferry

© Bradt Travel Guides Ltd

Lokrum

LOKRUM

Practical Information

THE CITY – ORIENTATION

Greater Dubrovnik spreads along the Dalmatian coast from the vast new suspension bridge crossing the outlet of the Rijeka Dubrovačka in the northwest to the desirable suburb of Ploče in the southeast, and across the Lapad and Babin Kuk peninsulas to the west.

The main harbour, Gruž, sits between the mainland and Babin Kuk. From here it's a 500m walk south along the quay to the central bus station; a further 2km south (a ten-minute bus ride) brings you to the old town. Opposite this, and accessible from the old port, is the island of Lokrum, where you'll find the nicest beaches. Dominating the whole town is the 412m Mount Srđ, with the Imperial Fort and a radio and TV mast sitting on top, and a huge commemorative cross.

The old town itself is incredibly compact – the vast walls which surround it are a whisper under 2km long, and the main street, Stradun (also known as Placa, pronounced *platsa*), which crosses the city, is barely 300m in length.

At the western end of Stradun is the Pile gate, outside which you'll find a taxi rank, the main bus stop for the old town, and tourist information. At the eastern end of Stradun is the belltower, and a winding street leading up to the Dominican Monastery and the Ploče gate. Outside this is another taxi rank, bus stop, and the road up to the Ploče hotels.

South of Stradun is the part of the town which was originally Roman. Here you'll find the cathedral, the Rector's Palace, St Blaise's Church and most of the monumental buildings. On the other side of Stradun, to the north, is the part of town which was originally Slav; narrow streets run steeply uphill to the landward walls, bisected by Prijeko, a narrow restaurant-filled lane running parallel to Stradun. Some of the streets in the old town don't have street numbers, but given the scale of the place this isn't usually a problem.

The majority of things you want to see and do are within the city walls, or close by. Accommodation on the other hand is for the most part well outside, either in Ploče or on Babin Kuk and Lapad; regular buses mean this isn't a problem.

WHEN TO VISIT

The months of July and August are easily the most popular with all types of visitor, and with the best weather, the famous Summer Festival and everyone in a holiday mood it's not hard to see why. On the other hand prices are significantly higher, the crowds can be oppressive and you do need to make sure you've planned your trip well in advance.

My personal favourite times for visiting Dubrovnik are May, June and September. The weather still tends to be excellent, school holidays aren't happening, the crowds are noticeably thinner and the town's just that bit more relaxed. Later into autumn it's still likely to be warm, but it can be wetter too; and in early spring the weather's distinctly variable, though the fine days far outnumber the cool ones.

In winter, Dubrovnik quietens down and becomes more of a town for the locals than one in search of the next tourist dollar. You still run into the occasional flood of visitors, usually in for the day off a cruise ship, but in the evenings the city recovers some of the quiet charm which no doubt first attracted visitors here. On the other hand you're more likely to get rained on – though alternating showers and sunshine are much more likely than days of steady drizzle.

Finally if you're planning trips to any of the outlying islands, bear in mind that from November until Easter (and sometimes right through to the beginning of May) they're not expecting you. That means accommodation can be hard or impossible to find and restaurants may be closed for the duration. If the weather's bad, you should seriously consider staying in town. Wandering round the old city on a wet or windy day isn't unpleasant at all; sitting in a howling gale on a windswept island, praying the ferry's going to come and that the ride home isn't too sickening, can be a truly miserable experience. On the other hand there's little to beat a day trip in fine winter weather to a place deserted of tourists, with a picnic and a bottle of wine in your knapsack.

HIGHLIGHTS

How much you get to see of Dubrovnik and the surrounding area will depend not only on how much time you have but also on whether you'll be able to drag yourself away from the old town. All too often I've visited with grand intentions to get out to far-flung islands and across the border into Bosnia or Montenegro and yet ended up spending practically my entire trip inside the city walls. It's simply that beguiling.

What to see in a single day

If you're here for just one day then you'll necessarily be limited to the old town – which is not the end of the world, as it's what everyone rightly comes for. The absolute must, if your legs are up to it, is the 2km walk around the city walls (see page 141), which gives not just wonderful views (including the one on the cover of this book) across the red roofs and stone houses of the old town but also a real sense of historical perspective.

Down in the town itself the most important things to visit are the Rector's Palace (see page 154), where the rector spent his month as head of state in virtual confinement, and the two monasteries at either end of town. Near the Pile gate you'll find the Franciscans (see page 161), with the old pharmacy and a fine set of cloisters as well as a brooding church. At the other end of the gorgeous polished marble main street, Stradun, and next to the Ploče gate, are the Dominicans (see page 162), with more cloisters, a small but interesting museum, and a church with a magnificent Byzantine crucifixion.

It's also pretty much obligatory to pop in at the city's other pair of main churches, either side of the Rector's Palace. In the cathedral (see page 164) there's not much to be amazed by in the building itself, but the treasury is really quite extraordinary, while in St Blaise's (see page

Stradun

166) the main attraction is the original statue of the town's patron saint over the altar, holding a pre-earthquake model of Dubrovnik.

In busily ticking off the sights, however, don't miss the main attraction, which is the old town itself. Take time to drift at random (it's impossible to get lost here) and soak up some of the atmosphere of times past. Wander out on to the old harbour and around the side of St John's fortress to where the city comes to an end and the sea begins in earnest. And don't forget to leave time to sample a handful of Dubrovnik's cafés and bars and at least one of its numerous restaurants.

Even on a day trip, you may also have time to visit the island of Lokrum (see page 175). Regular taxi boats make the 15-minute trip from the old harbour, and the views back to the city are splendid. Lokrum itself is a delight, offering rocks to swim from, shady woods, a dilapidated Napoleonic fort on the hill, and a café set in a ruined Benedictine monastery.

Two or three days

If you have more than a day in Dubrovnik then you may feel like venturing further afield – though it's just as likely you'll fall under the city's spell and be unable to leave. Even so, you should at least try and get as far as the island of Lokrum, just offshore.

If you do escape, an excellent half- or full-day trip can be had down the coast to the town of Cavtat (see page 184), which is only 20 minutes away by bus. It's really not much more than a fishing village, but the setting is lovely and there are several attractions which make the journey worthwhile – including a whole clutch of waterfront bars and restaurants. Up the coast 25km in the other direction is Trsteno (see page 211), with its marvellous 16th-century arboretum; well worth a couple of hours of your time and a welcome break from the crowds. It can be combined with a visit to the town of Ston (see page 212), 30km further on, with its old walls rising above the town practically rivalling Dubrovnik's, and the best oysters in Croatia.

Three days or more

With more time on your hands an island excursion is a great way of spending a day (or even two). The nearest inhabited islands to Dubrovnik are the Elaphites, which lie in a string northwest of the city. The nearest, Koločep (see page 191), is just half an hour away from Dubrovnik on the ferry, while the furthest, Šipan (see page 196), is the best part of two hours' distant. Between the two is Lopud (see page 192), the most developed and yet perhaps the loveliest of the three.

Further offshore still is the magical island of Mljet (see page 199), though with the new fast catamaran it's now only an hour or so from Dubrovnik. With lush vegetation, an abandoned monastery on an island on a lake, Europe's only wild mongooses and relatively few visitors, Mljet is a treasure not to be missed. The western end of the island is a national park, criss-crossed with forest paths and excellent for walkers or cyclists.

If you have the time and inclination, there's also great walking to be had back on the mainland, right next to Dubrovnik. There's a beautiful path running south with stunning views back to the old town, for example, or the slightly more strenuous track which goes all the way round the Babin Kuk peninsula (see page 182), emerging at the harbour of Gruž. Serious walkers for their part won't be able to resist the hike up to the summit of Srđ (see page 181), the mountain right behind Dubrovnik – and the views down from the 412m summit are truly remarkable.

Finally, if you really have plenty of time there are interesting day-trip possibilities south to Montenegro (see page 217) and east into Bosnia (see page 215).

TOUR OPERATORS
In the UK

There's a long history of package tourism as well as independent travel from the UK to Dubrovnik, and there are plenty of operators to choose from – beyond those listed below it's worth seeing what your local travel agent has to offer, as well as visiting www.visit-croatia.co.uk/touroperators and www.tourist-offices.org.uk/croatia/uktourops.html.

Balkan Holidays Tel: 020 7543 5555; fax: 020 7543 5577; www.balkanholidays.co.uk. Offers self-catering apartments and flights from London and Manchester.

Bond Tours Tel: 01372 745300; fax: 01372 749111; www.bondtours.com. Highly recommended. Offers city breaks as well as packages to the Elaphites and Mljet, and accommodation-only options.

Bridge Travel Tel: 0870 191 7185; www.bridge-travel.co.uk. Specialises in city breaks to Dubrovnik, year-round.

Cosmos Holidays Tel: 0800 093 3134; www.cosmos-holidays.co.uk. Claims to be the UK's largest independent tour operator; flights from London and Manchester.

Croatia For Travellers Tel: 020 7226 4460; fax: 020 7226 7906; www.croatiafortravellers.co.uk. Aimed squarely at independent travellers, they can tailor a holiday to your precise requirements, or just book you the flights and hotels you want.

First Choice Tel: 0870 576 8373; www.firstchoice.co.uk. Specialises in southern Dalmatia, with packages to Koločep and Cavtat as well as Dubrovnik. Also offers 'Exclusive top Dubrovnik Hotels' under its Sovereign Holidays brand. Flights from London and Manchester.

Headwater Holidays Tel: 01606 720099; fax: 01606 720034; www.headwater.com. Specialises in walking and sightseeing tours.

Hidden Croatia Tel: 020 7736 6066; fax: 020 7384 9347; www.hiddencroatia.com. Offers flights-only as well as tailor-made trips. Flights from London and Manchester.

Holiday Options Tel: 0870 013 0450; fax: 01444 242454; www.holidayoptions.co.uk. One of the biggest and best-known operators, with flights from London, Manchester, Birmingham, Norwich and Glasgow.

Mercian Travel Tel: 0870 036 8372; www.merciantravel.co.uk. Offers bridge and bowling holidays to the Dubrovnik riviera, year-round.

Original Travel Company Tel: 020 7978 7333; fax: 020 7978 7222; www.originaltravel.co.uk. Specialises in activity and exclusive holidays – including kayaking around the Elaphites.

Saga Holidays Tel: 0800 300 500; www.saga.co.uk. Aimed at the over-50s, Saga has a loyal following and offers flights from London and Manchester – though their website's a navigational nightmare.

Simply Croatia Tel: 020 8541 2214; fax: 020 8541 2280; www.simplytravel.co.uk. Offers individual packages to villas, small hotels etc. Flights from London and Manchester.

Thomson Lakes and Mountains Tel: 0870 606 1470; www.thomsonlakesandmountains.co.uk. A subsidiary of the UK's biggest tour operator, with flights from London and Manchester.

In North America

There are very few North American operators which list Dubrovnik as a package destination, though some of the bigger companies occasionally feature it – usually combined with neighbouring countries. An example is Adventures Abroad (tel: +1 800 665 3998 in the USA and Canada, +1 800 147 827 in Australia; www.adventures-abroad.com), which offers a small selection of itineraries featuring Croatia.

Otherwise you can contact the New York office of the Croatia National Tourist Board (tel: +1 212 279 8672; fax: +1 212 279 8683) – though a quicker route to a Croatian holiday can generally be had via one of the UK operators listed above. It may also be worth checking what's available with your local travel agent.

RED TAPE
Passports/visas

Nationals of most English-speaking (UK, Ireland, USA, Canada, Australia and New Zealand) and EU countries only need a valid passport to visit Croatia for up to three months; if you want to stay longer it's easier to leave the country and come back in again than it is to get an extension. If you don't need a visa for Croatia you shouldn't need one for hops across the border to neighbouring Bosnia & Herzegovina and Montenegro, which apply the same three-month visa exemption for tourists.

Full details of who does and doesn't need a visa for Croatia, as well as up-to-date addresses and phone numbers of all the Croatian diplomatic missions worldwide – and foreign diplomatic missions in Croatia – can be found on the Ministry of Foreign Affairs' website at www.mvp.hr.

Most English-speaking countries have consulates in the capital, Zagreb; the UK also maintains a consulate in Dubrovnik (at Buničeva poljana 3/I, 20000 Dubrovnik; tel/fax: +385 20 324 597; mob: 091 455 5325, open Mon, Tue, Thu, Fri, 10.00–13.00).

The addresses for the Croatian diplomatic missions in the main English-speaking countries are listed below.

Croatian diplomatic missions abroad

United Kingdom Embassy of the Republic of Croatia in the United Kingdom of Great Britain and Northern Ireland (also covers Ireland), 21 Conway St, London W1P 5HL; tel: +44 207 387 1144; fax: +44 207 387 0936; email: consular-dept@croatianembassy.co.uk

USA

Washington Embassy of the Republic of Croatia in the United States of America, 2343 Massachusetts Av, NW, Washington DC, 20008; tel: +1 202 588 5899; fax: +1 202 588 8937; email: public@croatiaemb.org.

Chicago Consulate General of the Republic of Croatia in the United States of America, 737 North Michigan Av, Suite 1030, Chicago, IL 60611; tel: +1 312 482 9902; fax: +1 312 482 9902; email: croatia@chicagonet.net.

Los Angeles Consulate General of the Republic of Croatia in the United States of America, 11 766 Wilshire Bd, Suite 1250, Los Angeles, CA 90025; tel: +1 310 477 1009; fax: +1 310 477 1866; email: croconla@aol.com.

New York Consulate General of the Republic of Croatia in the United States of America, 369 Lexington Av, New York, NY 10017; tel: +1 212 599 3066; fax: +1 212 599 3106; email: Croatian.consulate@gte.net.

St Paul, Minnesota Consulate General of the Republic of Croatia in the United States of America; tel: +1 612 429 4183, fax: +1 612 429 6079

Australia

Canberra Embassy of the Republic of Croatia in Australia (also covers New Zealand), 14 Jindalee Crescent, O'Malley Act, 2606, Canberra; tel: +61 2 6286 6988; fax: +61 2 6286 3544; email: croemb@dynamite.com.au.

Melbourne Consulate General of the Republic of Croatia in Australia, 9/24 Albert Rd, South Melbourne, 3205, Victoria; tel: +61 3 9699 2633, fax: +61 3 9696 8271; email: concro@labyrinth.com.au.

Perth Consulate General of the Republic of Croatia in Australia, St George's Terrace, Perth, 6831, Western Australia; PO Box Z5366; tel: +61 8 9321 6044; fax: +61 8 9321 6240; email: croconpe@iinet.net.au.

Sydney Consulate General of the Republic of Croatia in Australia, 4/379 Kent St, Sydney, 2001, New South Wales; tel: +61 2 9299 8899; fax: +61 2 9299 8855; email: cro_con_Sydney@speednet.com.au

Canada Embassy of the Republic of Croatia in Canada, 229 Chapel St, Ottawa, Ontario, KIN 7Y6; tel: +1 613 562 7820; fax: +1 613 562 7821; email: info@croatiaemb.net; www.croatiaemb.net

Ireland Embassy of the Republic of Croatia in Ireland, 22 Lower Rathmines Rd, Rathmines, Dublin 6; tel: +353 1 498 3018; fax: +353 1 498 3014

New Zealand Consulate General of the Republic of Croatia in New Zealand, 131 Lincoln Rd, Henderson/PO Box 83200, Edmonton, Auckland; tel: +64 9 836 5581; fax: +64 9 836 5481; email: cro-consulate@xtra.co.nz

Police registration

Croatian law stipulates that all visitors must register with the police within 24 hours of arrival. If you're staying in a hotel, hostel or campsite, or in a private room arranged through an agency, this will be done for you automatically.

If you're in a private room you've found for yourself, or you're staying with friends, then they're supposed to register you. This doesn't always happen – and unless you're picked up by the police, that shouldn't be a problem. Even if you are questioned, if it's clear you're a tourist then the police will usually just tick you off and make sure they know where you're staying. But if you've been unregistered for a while then you could be in trouble – and even deported.

Customs

There are no restrictions on the personal belongings you can bring into Croatia, though the government recommends you declare big-ticket items (boats, laptop computers, expensive camera or movie equipment etc) to be sure of being able to re-export them hassle-free. Coming into or out of Croatia by plane or boat, or crossing the border in your own non-Croatian (or Bosnian) registered vehicle, it's incredibly rare to be stopped or seriously questioned for any length of time.

Standard customs allowances apply for duty-free tobacco and alcohol – 200 cigarettes and one litre of spirits per person – and you're restricted to half a kilo of coffee, if that's your fix. If you're taking your pets then make sure they have an international veterinary certificate showing that it's been at least two weeks but not more than six months since they've been vaccinated.

You can take as much foreign currency as you want in and out of the country, but you can't export more than 2,000 kuna. For goods costing over 500 kuna you can claim a tax refund on the way out of Croatia on presentation of the tax cheque the merchant will have given you for this purpose – but it can be a grindingly long procedure. Any questions you have can be answered by the helpful staff at the Customs Administration in Zagreb (tel/fax: +385 1 610 2333).

GETTING THERE AND AWAY

There are four main ways of reaching Dubrovnik: by plane, boat, bus or car. You could conceivably be arriving by bicycle or on foot, but in that case you probably won't have room to be carrying this guide. You can't get to Dubrovnik by train as there isn't a railway line. Most visitors either fly or come in by sea, on a cruise ship, ferry, yacht or motor launch.

By plane

Flying to Dubrovnik is easily the quickest way of arriving – it's just two and a half hours from London. For details of airport transfers see page 87.

Both British Airways (www.britishairways.com) and Croatia Airlines (www.croatiaairlines.hr) fly to Dubrovnik, though not always every day, and in winter you may have to transit via Zagreb. Summer flights tend to be both direct and a good deal more frequent. Expect to pay anything between £200 and £500 for a scheduled return flight, including taxes.

For the time being there aren't any budget airlines serving Dubrovnik, though it can only be a matter of time (one hopes). There are charters, however, with First Choice (www.firstchoice.co.uk) offering flights from London Gatwick and Manchester; Hidden Croatia (Air Adriatic; www.hiddencroatia.com) from London Stansted and Manchester; Holiday Options (www.holidayoptions.co.uk) from London Gatwick, Manchester, Birmingham, Norwich and Glasgow; Newmarket Holidays (www.newmarket-group.co.uk) from London Gatwick, Belfast, Exeter,

Newcastle, Glasgow, Cardiff, Manchester, Edinburgh and Liverpool (but not in July and August, bizarrely); Palmair (tel: 01202 200700 – no website, apparently) from Bournemouth; Sunsail Holidays (www.sunsailflights.co.uk) from London Gatwick; and Thomas Cook (www.thomascook.com) from London Gatwick and Manchester.

There are no direct flights from the USA, Canada, Australia or New Zealand, but most airlines will be able to route you through a European hub, usually in conjunction with Croatia Airlines. Return tickets from New York to Dubrovnik start at under US$1,000 out of season, though they tend to rise to over US$1,500 in summer.

If you're having trouble finding a reasonably priced flight through the usual channels (newspapers, travel agents etc) there are a number of alternatives. One is to take a package tour – see the list of travel agents on page 47. Even if you want to sort out your own accommodation, some operators will be happy to arrange a 'flights-only' package for you. Even if this isn't the case, it can sometimes still work out cheaper to book yourself on a package and then not use the entire accommodation segment – though if you do this you should check the conditions very carefully to ensure you still have a return flight home. Charter operators flying to Dubrovnik from the UK are listed above.

You should also surf the internet, as it can be a great place to shop around for flights. UK websites such as www.cheapflights.co.uk, www.lastminute.co.uk, or www.travelocity.co.uk, or US sites like www.expedia.com or www.farebeater.com will give you a quick idea about what's really available and how much it costs. But don't imagine that just because it's on the internet it's necessarily the cheapest –

Getting there and away

you may find the fare in your local travel agent's window is still better. And the websites listed here don't cover low-cost carriers or charter operators.

By boat

Large numbers of visitors come to Dubrovnik by boat – on a cruise ship, a ferry or their own chartered yacht or motor-launch (for more information on sailing you'll need to get hold of my comprehensive book *Croatia: The Bradt Travel Guide*) – and it's a most agreeable way to arrive. The republic depended on maritime trade routes for its wealth over the centuries, and it's still today a largely seaward-facing city.

Overnight ferries come direct from Bari in Italy. Jadrolinija operates a service three to four times a week, as does Azzurra Line (www.agestea.com/azzurra-eng.htm). Jadrolinija also runs a service all the way down the Croatian coast from Rijeka to Dubrovnik, stopping in at Zadar, Split, Hvar and Korčula on the way – though the whole journey takes the best part of 24 hours.

For details of how to get between the port at Gruž, where all boats arrive (excepting the little taxi boats which run out to Lokrum and Cavtat and back), see page 87.

By bus

Most readers of this guide won't be coming into Dubrovnik for the first time by bus. Partly that's down to Dubrovnik's location a long way down a very long coastline, and partly it's because international bus travel isn't all that cheap any more. The journey from London takes at least two days each way and fares – without a student discount – start at around £120.

That said, you may be on a coach holiday – in which case your first view of Dubrovnik will be the fabulous, spanking-new suspension bridge over the Dubrovačka Rijeka inlet, which cuts a welcome 15km off the journey. From one side you'll notice it labelled as the *Tuđman Bridge*, while from the other it's the *Dubrovnik Bridge* – telling you something useful about local politics.

For information on Dubrovnik's local buses, and long-distance buses within Croatia, see pages 88 and 92.

By car

Dubrovnik's not a great city to come to by car. It's a very long way (2,175km from London) and once there you can't park – or at the very least parking is a major hassle (see page 93). What's more, the city's easily manageable without a car, either on foot or using public transport.

On the other hand, if you're touring around the country – especially with a family – it's quite understandable that you want to have your own vehicle with you. In this case it might be worth considering staying somewhere out of town for the Dubrovnik part of your trip – such as Cavtat, for example (see page 184) – and then coming in on day trips on the bus or a local ferry.

If you're mainly interested in southern Dalmatia it may also be worth looking at fly/drive packages, as getting your car to Dubrovnik is both time-consuming and expensive (in terms of fuel and tolls) whichever way you go. Some day there will be a fast road down the coast from Split, but for the time being the single-lane **Magistrala** (named after Marshal Tito) is all there is – and inevitably it clogs up badly in summer.

The most important thing to remember, if you are driving, is to stay within the law. You may find Croatian drivers rather ambitious – to the extent that blind corners and oncoming traffic aren't seen as a natural impediment to overtaking – but don't be too competitive; the omnipresent (and omnipotent) traffic police are quick to keep drivers in line with steep fines (and worse).

Speed limits – 50km/h in built-up areas; 90km/h out of town (locally highly variable; keep your eyes peeled) – are strictly enforced, and there are an astonishing number of speed traps, especially along the Magistrala. Foreigners, rightly or wrongly, attract police attention. If you are stopped for a traffic violation, you may find the police ready to negotiate a lower penalty with you – the heavier fine for speeding, for example, might be traded down to the lower fine (payable in cash) for not wearing your seatbelt.

Turning into a one-way street the wrong way in Gruž, I was immediately stopped by the police, and told to park the car in a spot reserved for the disabled. I was then given a choice of having my licence taken away and a 1,500 kuna fine (for driving the wrong way down a one-way street – unmarked as such, I might add), or paying the 150 kuna fine for parking in a disabled spot. I'll leave you to guess which I chose.

In the event of an accident or breakdown you can call the Croatian Automobile Club's hotline by dialling 987. If you see someone *else* in need of assistance you're legally obliged to stop and help. And remember that it's illegal for drunks or children under the age of 12 to sit in the front of the car. The drink-driving limit, previously 50mg/100ml, was changed in 2004 to zero tolerance.

To source car parts or fix problems your first port of call should be a petrol station (usually open from dawn until dusk; fuel costs around 7 kuna per litre). It's better, however, not to break down; parts may be in better supply and repairs may be more quickly effected than they used to be, but it can still be a costly and lengthy business.

TOURIST INFORMATION AND MAPS

You can get a great deal of information before you arrive from both the National Tourist Board and the local one in Dubrovnik – both publish a range of brochures, accommodation details and maps, and they have websites at www.croatia.hr and http::/web.tzdubrovnik.hr respectively. If you don't have easy access to the internet you can contact one of the following offices for more information:

Head office Croatian National Tourist Board, Iblerov trg 10/IV, Zagreb; tel: +385 1 469 9333; fax: +385 1 455 7827; email: info@htz.hr

UK office Croatian National Tourist Office, 162–164 Fulham Palace Rd, London W6 9ER; tel: +44 208 563 7979; fax: +44 208 563 2616; email: info@cnto.freeserve.co.uk

USA office Croatian National Tourist Office, Inc, 350 Fifth Av, Suite 4003, New York 10118; tel: +1 212 279 8672/+1 212 279 8674; fax: +1 212 279 8683; email: cntony@earthlink.net

(These are the only English-language offices for the National Tourist Board. For other European regional offices see www.croatia.hr and look within

'Representative Offices Abroad', under the home page – then look under the 'Contact' button at the bottom of the page.)

Dubrovnik office Dubrovnik Tourist Board, Cvijete Zuzorić 1/II, 20000 Dubrovnik; tel/fax: +385 20 323 887; email: info@tzdubrovnik.hr

Once in Dubrovnik you'll find tourist information at the official tourist office (see page 76) or at local tour operators, who are generally happy enough to help you out with information and street plans – though their real mandate is to find you accommodation and get you booked on to excursions.

As far as maps are concerned, there are about half a dozen different ones in circulation, mostly with the old town on one side and the surrounding city on the other. Given the modest size and scale of the place any of these should be more than adequate – which is just as well as I haven't yet come across a really professional map of the city and surrounds (accurately to scale, or marking footpaths, for example; but I cavil).

HEALTH

A reciprocal agreement between the EU countries and Croatia means that in theory EU citizens shouldn't have to pay for public hospital care – but in practice you may well be told that the service you need isn't available, and that you can only obtain it privately. Don't expect this to be any cheaper than it would be at home – in other words, make sure you have health insurance for major emergencies.

For minor treatments, a visit to a pharmacy (*ljekarna*) should sort you out – and there's very often someone who speaks some English. For more serious problems get yourself to the hospital (*bolnica*). Details of both can be found in the next chapter, on page 85.

You don't need any vaccinations for Croatia, though it's good to be up to date on tetanus with diphtheria and hepatitis A vaccine. On the whole it is safe to drink the water, if it's from any kind of public supply. If in doubt buy bottled water or purify by boiling or adding iodine either as drops or tablets.

If you are planning to travel outside Dubrovnik to rural areas during the summer months then be aware of a disease called tick-borne encephalitis (TBE). TBE, as the name suggests, is transmitted by the bite of an infected tick. They live in long grass and on the branches of overhanging trees and can drop on the unwary and go unnoticed unless you check your body and head afterwards. Sensible precautions include wearing trousers tucked into boots, hats and using tick repellents. Vaccination against TBE is preferred where possible, but there have been problems obtaining the vaccine in the UK more recently. Do not worry if you cannot get vaccinated before travel. Follow the advice above and carefully remove any ticks from your body and seek medical advice promptly, as it is still possible to receive treatment after exposure.

If you use needles for any reason you should bring a doctor's note explaining why, and if you wear contact lenses or glasses, bring spares; repairs and replacements aren't a problem, but can take time. If you're coming for an extended visit it does no harm to have a doctor's and dentist's check-up before you go – far easier at home than abroad.

Common problems

You're less resistant to disease abroad, so make sure your diet contains enough vitamins – and take supplements if you're not sure. Drink bottled water if you think the source is suspect – though publicly supplied water in Dubrovnik is fine. Do drink plenty of (non-alcoholic) liquids; it's easy to get dehydrated wandering around a sunny city that's full of heat-reflecting stone, and abundant in tempting cafés and bars.

You may also want to bring with you a mild laxative and something for diarrhoea, although both problems can normally be fixed with a change in diet (soft fruit for the first; dry-skinned fruit for the second). If you are afflicted with diarrhoea your biggest danger is dehydration, so make sure you drink plenty – soft still drinks are best.

Even if you're not heading out to the islands, it's a good idea to bring along a small supply of sticking plasters (Band-aids), antiseptic cream and mild painkillers (aspirin or paracetamol) – you can top up your supplies of these at any pharmacy.

From May onwards you should also think about protecting yourself against mosquitoes. All you'll need is a gizmo which plugs into a wall socket at night – you can buy these easily enough whenever mosquitoes are about.

Finally, don't hesitate to see a pharmacist or doctor if you're even slightly unsure about a diagnosis or cure. Know your source if you need a blood transfusion – HIV/AIDS is less prevalent in Croatia than in many countries, but you can't be too careful.

INSURANCE

Even on a weekend break, travel/health insurance is a good idea – it's reassuring to know you can be flown home if necessary. Read your policy's fine print and make sure it covers what you'll be doing. A general policy, covering health, theft and third-party insurance, is usually cheaper and less hassle than multiple policies, though you may find you're already covered for some or all of the risks by existing insurance (such as private healthcare, which sometimes includes foreign travel, or that provided to holders of credit cards).

If you need to claim, you'll have to provide supporting evidence in the form of medical bills, in the case of health, or a police statement, in the case of theft. Obtaining the latter can be tediously hard work, but essential if you're hoping for reimbursement.

Travel policies are issued by banks, travel agents and others, and it's worth shopping around amongst reputable providers, as the price varies considerably. Arrange for the insurance to cover your full journey time, and keep the policy safe with your other travel documents.

SAFETY

Croatia – and Dubrovnik in particular – is safer and freer of crime than most places in the EU, though it's common sense here as elsewhere not to be showy with money, jewellery or flashy possessions, and to keep your valuables close to you and separate from the rest of your luggage.

Safety

You'll see lots of police around, and they have rather fearsome powers – freedom of dissension shouldn't be taken for granted. The police carry out occasional spot checks on locals and foreigners alike for identification, so make sure you have your passport or identity card with you at all times. Otherwise you'll find the police friendly and helpful – though not all speak English.

If you do get arrested, stay courteous, even (especially) when it's difficult to do so. Stand, rather than sit, if you can (it puts you on an even footing), and establish eye contact – if you can do so without being brazen or offensive about it. Some people recommend shaking hands with officialdom, but it depends very much on the circumstances. Wait until an interpreter arrives (or anyone who understands you clearly) rather than be misunderstood. And remember that you can be held at a police station for up to 24 hours without being charged. Your consulate will be informed of your arrest, normally within the first day.

Sexual harassment

Dubrovnik is safe for women travellers, though like anywhere with a big influx of holidaymakers it has its fair share of local men on the make. This tends to come in the form of courteous persistence rather than aggression, and is usually easily rebuffed. Speaking firmly – in any language – should make your intentions clear.

People dress here the same way as they do anywhere in Europe, so there's nothing to worry about as far as dressing modestly is concerned – though wandering around churches in beachwear is likely to offend. If you want to get your kit off, the nearest naturist beach is on Lokrum (see page 175) – and you won't be pestered here.

Important telephone numbers
The chances are you'll never need them, but here are three phone numbers worth knowing: 92 for the police, 93 for fire and 94 for an ambulance.

WHAT TO TAKE
The best way for packing for anywhere – and Dubrovnik's no exception – is to set out all the things you think you'll need and then take only about a third. How much you eventually end up taking will depend to a large extent on how long you're going for and whether you have your own transport (everyone takes more in their own car). But be realistic, especially if you're going to have to carry all your own stuff.

If you're planning on using the beaches, remember that they're not sandy here, so bring appropriate beach footwear – along with the usual hat, sunglasses, suncream etc. Summer evenings can be cool but are rarely cold, so a light sweater should be sufficient – but if you're coming here in winter bring some warm clothes and a waterproof.

Don't forget the usual range of documents you'll need – passport, tickets, travellers' cheques, cash, insurance papers, credit card, driving licence – and something to carry them in. A belt-bag or pouch is practical, but also draws attention to where you're keeping your valuables; I prefer a zipped pocket for the essentials, whether that's in a daypack or trousers, but it's a personal choice. Bring any books you want to read – though you can also pick up papers a few days old and the usual range of pulp fiction in English here too.

Finally, bring spare glasses if you wear them, along with any special medicines you need. You may also find it handy to have a tube of travel detergent with you for rinsing out your smalls, and a travel alarm for those early starts. And last but not least, if you're bringing any electrical appliances – even just a hairdryer or a phone charger – remember an adaptor. Croatian sockets are the same round two-pinned variety you find all across Europe.

MONEY

Since May 1994, Croatia's currency has been the kuna – literally a marten, named after the trade in marten skins in Roman times, and first struck as a Croatian coin in 1256. It's one of the few currencies in the world still officially named after an animal (the American 'buck' was never legal tender – even if it's still in fashion an awful long time since trading in deerskins was a measure of anything in the USA).

The kuna (HRK is the international three-letter code) is divided up into 100 lipa (literally lime tree, or linden). There are 1, 2, 5, 10, 20 and 50 lipa coins, 1, 2 and 5 kuna coins, and 5, 10, 20, 50, 100, 200, 500 and 1,000 kuna banknotes. There's also a 25 kuna coin, but the chances are you'll never see one. On the whole, people aren't comfortable with the two largest notes, and you may have trouble breaking them – ask for 100s and 200s when you're changing money.

The euro has also increasingly been used as a parallel currency – the vast majority of Dubrovnik's visitors switched to the euro at the beginning of 2002. Most people are comfortable with euro pricing, and you can pay with euros almost everywhere – but don't necessarily expect the right (or complete) change. You're much better off changing enough money for a couple of days at a time and getting used to the kuna. The kuna is pretty stable, averaging around 7.60 to the euro and 11 to the English pound.

Finding a place to buy kuna is a doddle – all banks, exchange offices and post offices, and most travel agencies and hotels will happily let you turn in your money, though you're better off with euros or sterling than US dollars, as there are so many dollar forgeries in circulation. Exchange rates are (remarkably) almost the same wherever you choose to change your money – fractionally worse at hotels, perhaps, but the difference is minimal.

Major credit cards (notably Visa, Eurocard/Mastercard and American Express) are accepted by most big hotels, restaurants and shops, though if you're staying in private rooms (see page 108) you'll find cash is king (kuna or euros). Credit cards can also be used for raiding cash dispensers; they tend to take Visa or Eurocard, but not both.

Money is safest brought in the form of travellers' cheques, which are worth the small commission you pay for the peace of mind. You lose about the same percentage of your money if you use a credit card, but it's easier to keep track of cheques. American Express cheques are still the most widely used, easily recognised and most quickly refunded in case of loss or theft, and your local bank back home can issue them to you (though you may have to insist).

Finally, have enough money/resources with you – getting more wired to you from home is both expensive and a hassle.

BUDGETING

How much you'll spend will depend on what level of luxury you're looking for, and to some extent on the season. Camping and using public transport is going to cost a lot less than staying in swanky hotels and cabbing it to and from the old town. That said, Dubrovnik is neither particularly cheap nor expensive – broadly speaking you should expect to pay about the same as in western Europe. Hotel accommodation and restaurants are on average cheaper than in the UK, but about the same as in France – though house wine is considerably cheaper than in either. Supermarket prices on the other hand are slightly higher than they would be in the UK.

After the cost of getting to Croatia, your biggest single expense will be accommodation. Expect to pay from €40 to €100 per night for a double room in private accommodation in summer, while doubles in hotels start at around €60 and go right up to €500 (room prices are always quoted in euros, though paid in kuna). Single rooms are relatively scarce, but when available go for about 70% of the cost of a double. Off season some establishments (both hotels and private rooms) will discount by up to 20% in spring and autumn, and as much as 50% in winter.

For a couple, daily food and drink costs from around 250 kuna for picnic food bought in supermarkets and maybe one meal a day in a cheap restaurant or pizzeria, without wine, to 600 kuna for breakfast in a café and lunch and dinner with wine in slightly more upmarket restaurants. An average grill-type restaurant meal for two, with salad, skewers of meat, and wine, averages around 100 kuna a head. A slap-up fish dinner at a smart restaurant on the other hand can easily set two of you back 750 kuna or more.

Public transport is inexpensive by EU standards, with a single-zone bus ticket going for 10 kuna, while the bus from Dubrovnik to Korčula (which takes four hours and includes the ferry) costs just 80 kuna.

If you're really eking out the cash (camping, picnic food) you could get away with a budget of 150 kuna per person per day. Twice that would get you into private rooms and cheap restaurants, while 450 kuna would buy you a nice holiday, but not fish every day. For that, and upper-end hotels, you'd need to count on 750 kuna per person per day – and of course you can always spend more…

Entry fees for attractions are reasonably inexpensive, but in a constant state of flux, so don't be surprised if the prices here have changed – they were correct at the time of writing (summer 2004), when you could expect to pay 5 kuna to see the treasury in Dubrovnik Cathedral or 30 kuna to walk around the old town walls.

BUSINESS/TIME

Most businesses officially operate from 08.30 to 16.30, Monday to Friday. If you're calling ahead of your journey – or having people call you in Dubrovnik – remember that it operates on Central European Time (CET). That's an hour ahead of GMT, six hours ahead of New York and Washington, nine hours ahead of California, and eight hours behind Sydney and Melbourne (ten in the European winter). Summertime dates in Dubrovnik are the same as in most of the rest of Europe, with the clocks going forward an hour in spring and back an hour in autumn.

The working environment – dress, culture etc – is similar to that in most European countries, but if you're doing business don't be surprised if you're expected to cement deals or friendships with a shot (or several) of *rakija* or *travarica* (see page 116). If you don't drink out of choice, you need to invent a good reason why – the culture isn't particularly tolerant of non-drinkers.

OPENING TIMES

Croats are industrious and hard-working, but like to knock off early and enjoy the evening. So you'll find people up at dawn, and many offices and shops open from 07.30 or even 07.00, but you may well find businesses shut after 16.00. Supermarkets and pharmacies have fairly long hours, and tend to be open all day, while smaller shops may take an extended lunch hour.

Generally speaking, things tend to be open when they're needed – if there's a real demand then it'll be met. Travel agents open from early in the morning until late at night, seven days a week, in summer, but may well only open in the morning and on weekdays for the rest of the year. The 08.00–11.00 slot is far and away the most reliable time, year-round, if you want to be sure of finding something open.

Museums are also almost always open in the morning, but some close at 13.00 or 14.00 – so again, your sightseeing should be programmed around morning visits followed by a late lunch. Opening times are sometimes extended in summer – but not always.

Some churches are only opened for church services, and the periods just before and after them. If there's something you absolutely must see, which is closed, the tourist office may be able to help you find the person with the key.

PHOTOGRAPHY

Dubrovnik sometimes seems like it was designed to be photographed – with fine weather, gorgeous light, lots of great perspectives and a blissfully traffic-free old town.

With a long history of tourism, you're unlikely to run into people-problems with photography in Dubrovnik – they're used to it – but that doesn't mean you shouldn't apply the usual ethical standards. Respect privacy, don't take pictures you know will offend, and especially don't take pictures when you're asked not to.

Digital photography is increasingly popular – but bear in mind the usual limitations of memory size, battery life etc, and know your camera well. In spite of their point-and-shoot reputation, it's still quite hard to get really first-class pictures with digital cameras unless you've gone the professional route and bought a top-range digital SLR.

If you're using standard equipment it's worth noting that, while print film is easily available (if a bit more expensive than at home), slide film is relatively hard to find – especially if you have a particular brand preference. If you're buying film check the use-by date; some of the rolls you see for sale expired years ago. Finally, take films home for processing.

CULTURAL DOS AND DON'TS

All visitors have an effect not just on the place they're visiting but on its people too. There are numerous arguments for and against this which don't need to be enumerated here – suffice it to say that it's worth considering both the environmental and social effects of your visit.

Environment

Dubrovnik's environment is in good shape, so don't spoil it – preserving it is in everyone's interest.

The biggest impact you personally can have on the environment is to start a fire on one of the islands. There's almost nothing that can be done once a fire's out of control, as the forests tend to be tinder-dry in summer. Indeed, unless there's a plentiful supply of water close by, it's advisable to avoid fires (or even naked flames) altogether.

Litter, by comparison, is a simple question of ugliness. Dubrovnik's old town is cleaned every day, but that's no excuse for not finding a bin to put your litter in. Out of town, where stuff won't necessarily be picked up by the authorities, the issue is even more important. Paper tissues take months to deteriorate, orange peel positively glows, and tin cans always look horrible. So take your litter with you – and if you collect any you find along the way you can feel suitably saintly about yourself.

If you're in the wilds, and you can't find a toilet, do at least bury your doings – there are few sights (or sensations) more unpleasant than coming across someone else's.

Dress/naturism

In summer you won't look out of place in shorts and a T-shirt, but you won't be welcome in churches if you're too skimpily dressed. Seaside topless sunbathing won't usually offend, but you shouldn't really be anywhere off the beach in your swimsuit (or indeed out of it).

Since Croatia is the main homing ground for the great European naturist – and hundreds of thousands come every year just to get their kit off here – you're never that far from a naturist beach. The island of Lokrum, all of 15 minutes away, is the nearest to Dubrovnik. Naturist beaches are usually marked by 'FKK' signs.

Croatia's also the only country I've ever been to where you can go on a naturist sailing holiday. If that's your predilection, mind your tackle.

Gay/lesbian

Homosexuality may have been legalised a generation ago in Croatia, but you won't find people particularly tolerant or open about it. The country's first-ever gay parade wasn't held until June 2002, in Zagreb, and only a few hundred people took part – heavily protected from hecklers by a slew of riot police.

Most activity is still very much underground, and there isn't any kind of gay/lesbian scene at all in Dubrovnik, one of Croatia's most tolerant and liberal cities. Same-sex couples (men in particular) can still raise eyebrows (or even hackles) when checking into hotels. How you handle this will of course be up to you – some may be happy with a plausible cover story; others may find this stance too hypocritical.

As everywhere, younger people tend to be more tolerant than their elders.

Drugs

Illegal drugs are best avoided. They're available, but the penalties are stiff, and harsher still for smuggling – and don't for heaven's sake be tempted or tricked into carrying anything illegal across borders.

Tipping

A service charge isn't included in your restaurant bill, so – assuming the service has been good – it's appropriate to round up to the nearest 10 kuna or so. Don't be afraid not to tip if you think the service has been terrible, but equally don't be stingy – waiting staff in Dubrovnik aren't as well off as you are. Taxi drivers the world over expect fares to be rounded up, and those in Dubrovnik are no exception.

INTERACTING WITH LOCAL PEOPLE/GIVING SOMETHING BACK

Dubrovnik has been affected hugely by tourism, which has brought an improved standard of living to almost everyone. Tourism has also destroyed a way of life which was poorer and harsher, and yet, paradoxically, is often fondly remembered.

Your surly, inattentive waiter at the dog-end of the summer season is probably dreaming of being the fisherman his father was – even though he knows how hard a fisherman's life really is. Don't expect to be able to unravel this contradiction.

It's difficult in Dubrovnik itself – with the locals all too aware of the here-today gone-tomorrow nature of most visitors – to build bridges. But as everywhere it's worth making the effort to take the time to talk to chance acquaintances and share in a cup of coffee, or a drink and a cigarette, if invited. That said, it's a good idea not to discuss the recent war. It's a conversational minefield, and the last thing you want to do is step on a conversational landmine. Opinions amongst local people are sufficiently divergent on the subject for it to be a dangerous one to bring up. The only really safe thing you can say, if you're asked directly, is that you're pleased it's all over, and that peace should bring prosperity.

After travelling to Dubrovnik (and possibly even before you go) you may also want to do something for the community. After asking around when I was in town and extensive searches on the internet, I'm sorry to have to say that I was unable to find any voluntary programmes operating in the area – but if you know of any please drop me a line. I also drew a blank with charities, other than the Washington DC-based 'Rebuild Dubrovnik Fund' which seems to have successfully done its job.

Practicalities

TOURIST INFORMATION

The main official tourist office is 200m up the hill from the Pile gate, on the left-hand side, at Ante Starčićeva (formerly Maršala Tita) 7 (tel: 427 591; email: ured.pile@tzdubrovnik.hr; open Mon–Fri 09.00–19.00 and Sat 09.00–13.00). They dish out maps and various leaflets and can help you with booking concert tickets etc, and the office handily co-locates with an internet café (see page 84). There's been talk for years of the main office moving inside the old town walls, but at the time of writing it was still just talk.

There are two smaller, subsidiary tourist offices, one actually in the old town, at Miha Pracata (the eighth street on the right off Stradun, coming from Pile), with the same hours as above, and the other at Gruž, next door to the Jadrolinija ticket office, which has similar but less regular hours. You can also usually pick up maps and flyers from the various local tourist operators and agencies, though of late – particularly when a cruise ship arrives – they've taken to charging a token fee for maps.

If you need to register a complaint about anything to do with tourist facilities, the number to call is 351 048.

LOCAL TOUR OPERATORS AND TRAVEL AGENCIES

There are around 30 local tour operators and travel agencies in Dubrovnik; of these the following are the best-known and longest-established. They can organise entire holidays for you, including travel to and from your home country, as well as excursions and accommodation. Also included in the list is Dubrovnik's Croatia Airlines office.

Argosytours Lichtensteineov put 9; tel: 331 004; fax: 331 187; www.argosytours.hr. Dubrovnik-based operator specialising in Dubrovnik itself – but a bit out of the way, on Lapad.

Atlas Four local branches, including one just outside the Pile gate; tel: 442 574; fax: 442 570; www.atlas-croatia.com. Dubrovnik-based company which has been around since 1923, offering everything from tailor-made holidays to coach tours to flights to accommodation. Atlas also owns the Villa Argentina and Villa Orsula hotels in Ploče, and the island of Mljet's only hotel, the Odisej.

Croatia Airlines Right outside the Pile gate; tel: 413 777; fax: 413 993; www.croatiaairlines.hr. The national airline, with great-value domestic flights if you reserve and pay for them within Croatia – the catch being that you need to do so a long way ahead.

Generalturist Frana Supila 9; tel: 432 974; fax: 423 554; www.generalturist.com. Like Atlas, founded in 1923, although since 1999 it's been owned by Diners Club. This branch is just outside the Ploče gate.

Turistički Informativni Centar Stradun; tel: 323 350; fax: 323 351; www.tic-stradun.hr. The agency that most people think is the official tourist office – partly because of the name and partly because of the unbeatable location, right on the corner of Stradun, opposite the

Franciscan church, as you come in through the Pile gate. Specialises in excursions and private accommodation.

BANKS

There are over a dozen banks and nearly 30 ATMs in Dubrovnik, so you shouldn't have any trouble finding one. One of the biggest, with several branches, is the home-grown Dubrovačka Banka, which has a convenient branch right on Stradun with long opening hours. Current exchange rates are posted daily at all banks.

Dubrovačka Banka Stradun (Placa) 16; tel/fax: 321019. Open Mon–Fri 07.30–20.00, Sat 07.30–13.00.

MEDIA AND COMMUNICATIONS

Croatia has a surprisingly vigorous and wide-ranging press – though it's only very recently that the main newspapers, TV and radio stations have been anything other than a mouthpiece for the state.

Communications also suffered from the heritage of state communism, but a rapid uptake of mobile telephony and the internet means Croatia now has services worthy of its status as an EU supplicant. Electricity comes in the European-standard size and shape, at 220V and 50Hz, via standard European twin round-pinned sockets.

Media

Croatian independence in 1991 did little to bring freedom to the media, and it's only since the election of Stipe Mesić (in February 2000) that any real efforts have been made to liberate editors and journalists from half a century of government puppet-hood. Since then the president himself has spoken out in favour of keeping the media free from politics, and has encouraged journalists to practise their profession independently, as public servants rather than government acolytes.

The dominant media player is Croatian Radio and Television, HRT, which attracts an audience in excess of two million a day to its three TV channels and its national and local radio stations. HRT 1 and 2 produce the usual mix of news, documentaries, entertainment and game shows, while HRT 3 is dedicated almost exclusively to sport. The website, at www.hrt.hr, has an English-language site-map which will help you find the various web-streamed audio services on offer – useful for helping learn Croatian.

The most important daily newspaper is *Vjesnik* (online at www.vjesnik.com), which until recently was about as dry and unbiased as Russia's TASS in pre-Gorbachev days. With a change of management after the 2000 elections, the paper seems to be finding its independence – though it can still be heavy going.

Right at the other end of the publishing spectrum is the weekly *Feral Tribune*, which even uses a cod *Herald Tribune* masthead (see www.feral.hr). Originally a satirical supplement to Dalmatia's largest daily, *Slobodna Dalmacija*, before the mother paper was closed down by the government in 1992, *Feral Tribune* gradually became more serious, and was a regular thorn in the side of the Tuđman government.

For news in English your options are fairly limited. You can tune in to the BBC World Service on a short-wave radio, or – if you're lucky – catch one of the intermittent English-language news bulletins on HRT radio. You can also get the main English papers a day or two (or more) out of date. Otherwise the internet's your best bet, either by going through one of the two biggest Croatian news portals at www.hinet.hr or www.hic.hr, or by tuning in directly to the BBC or another English-language news provider (news.bbc.co.uk, www.cnn.com, abcnews.go.com, etc).

Post

Mail out of the former Yugoslavia used to take anything from two weeks to three months and, frankly, post out of 21st-century Croatia isn't all that much better – postcards within Europe tend to drift home in around two to three weeks, while airmail letters are quicker, but not enormously so. Just occasionally, something slips through a hole in the space–time continuum – a letter once arrived home in three days, and a card I sent to Australia once got there in eight – but you should reckon on post being fairly slow unless you pay for a premium, guaranteed-delivery service.

Post offices (*pošta*, or HPT) have long opening hours (see opposite). Parcels are reasonably cheap to send, but don't seal them until you've given the cashier time to check you're not posting bombs or contraband. If you send anything valuable you may have to pay duty on it when you get home.

If you want mail sent to you, have it addressed to Poste Restante, Pošta, 20108 Dubrovnik, if you want to collect it in the old town, otherwise Poste Restante, Pošta,

20000 Dubrovnik, if you want it to go to the main post office. If your family name is underlined and/or in capitals your mail is more likely to be filed correctly – but if there's nothing for you it's always worth asking them to look under your first name as well. Incoming post takes around ten days from most European destinations, and about two weeks from North America – but can be quicker, or indeed slower.

Stamps (*marke*) are also sold at news stands, tobacconists and anywhere you can buy postcards, which can save you queuing at the post office. In 2004 it cost 3.50 kuna to send a postcard to Europe, and 7 kuna to send one to Australia.

Main Post Office Put Republike 32 (just up from the bus station), 20000, Dubrovnik; tel: 413 960; fax: 413 962; open Mon–Fri 07.00–20.00, Sat 08.00–16.00, Sun 08.00–12.00.
Old Town, Široka 8, 20108, Dubrovnik; tel: 323 427; fax: 323 422; open Mon–Fri 08.00–19.00, Sat 08.00–14.00.

There are also post offices outside both main gates, which are open on weekdays 08.00–14.00, where you can usually find shorter queues. The one outside Pile is on the right-hand side of the road, just above the Hilton Imperial; the one outside Ploče is on the left-hand side as you head up towards the Hotel Excelsior.

Phone

The telephone network has vastly improved in the last 15 years, and you'll no longer need multiple attempts to reach the outside world. The international access code is 00, so for international calls simply dial 00 followed by your country code

WRONG NUMBER?

There's nothing worse than buying a guidebook and then finding out some of the phone numbers are wrong – but the sad truth is that (even though every single number is checked before going to print) numbers do change. So what to do? Your best option when we fail you (my apologies) is to log on to **www.htnet.hr/imenik**, Croatia's outstanding online phone directory. There's an English-language option, and it's fast and accurate. Another option is to call the tourist office – assuming their number hasn't changed.

(+44 for the UK, +1 for the USA and Canada, +61 for Australia and +64 for New Zealand) followed by the local phone number (without the leading zero in most cases, but not in Italy or Russia, for example).

The international code for calls into Croatia is +385 and the area code for Dubrovnik and the whole of southern Dalmatia is 020.

Phone boxes are plentiful, and operated by 25- to 500-unit phonecards, with the 25-unit card costing 15 kuna and the 100-unit card costing 40 kuna in the summer of 2004. Local calls normally cost one unit, with long-distance calls being quite a bit more expensive, especially at peak time (Monday to Saturday, 07.00–22.00). You can buy phonecards at post offices and news stands. For international calls of any duration you may prefer to phone from a post office, where you'll be allocated a metered phone and charged after the call. International calls mostly aren't exorbitant, but it does depend on the destination.

The people of Dubrovnik, like most Europeans, have gone mobile-mad, and well over half the population has a mobile phone. The network is comprehensive and the local operators have roaming agreements with their foreign counterparts, so you should find your own phone works – as long as you're on GSM. If you're using your own mobile, however, remember that international calls will be expensive and local ones even more so – you'll be calling from Croatia to home and back again, and paying for both segments.

If you're going to be glued to the phone, one option is to buy a local pre-paid subscription and then top up your SIM card as needed – if you do this, keep the SIM card for your home subscription in a safe place. Not only is a local pre-paid number convenient for your outgoing calls, but it also means you can easily be called from home.

A local pre-paid subscription can be bought at any phone shop or post office – the Simpa SIM card from Cronet costs just 298 kuna, which includes your first 100 kuna-worth of calls, after which top-up cards cost 50, 100 and 200 kuna. There are three local GSM operators, Vipnet (prefix 091), Cronet (098) and Mobitel (099); they all offer much the same deal and full network coverage.

One final word about phones – like everywhere else in the world, you should aim to avoid calling long distance or international from your hotel room. Tariffs for fixed and mobile calls may have fallen, but hotel rates certainly haven't. The cost of a 15-minute call home from a decent hotel room can spoil your entire trip.

Some useful phone numbers:

Emergencies

92	Police	431 777	Dubrovnik hospital
93	Fire	985	Public emergency centre
94	Ambulance	987	Roadside assistance

General

060 300 300	Croatia Airlines	418 000	Jadrolinija ferries
773 377	Čilipi airport	060 520 520	Weather forecast
357 088	Central bus station	9864	Exchange rates
357 020	City buses		

Telecoms

901	International operator	981	General information
902	International directory enquiries	988	Local operator
		989	Long-distance operator

Internet

Internet uptake has been rapid in Croatia, and there's an enormous amount of information available online (see page 232). Where it's been slower on the uptake is in the regular use of email. While some people are instantly responsive, many won't answer an initial email. During the research for this book, many hundreds of emails were sent, the vast majority into the void. The frustrating thing is that when you do follow up with a phone call, the first response is all too often: 'Ah, yes, we saw your email'!

Dubrovnik has several internet cafés, with hourly online fees coming in at anything from 20 to 40 kuna. New establishments have a tendency to open and close at dizzying intervals, and you'll find places off Prijeko which are distinctly informal (more of a bar with a spare terminal or a gaming centre than a place you might go to do business). The three listed here were all bona fide and operational in the summer of 2004.

Dubrovnik Internet Centar Ante Starčićeva 7; daily 09.00–22.00. In the same building as the main tourist office.
DU Net Put Republike 7; open Mon–Sat 08.00–16.00. Just up from the bus station, in the same building as the Raiffeisenbank Austria.
Narodna knjižnica – Internet centar Od Puča 6; open Mon–Fri 08.00–20.00, Sat 08.00–13.00. In the old town, on the same street as the Pučić Palace hotel.

HOSPITAL AND PHARMACIES

Dubrovnik's **General Hospital** (*Opća bolnica*) is up on Lapad, and as you'd expect the accident and emergency service works 24 hours a day (tel: 431 777; fax: 426 149; call 94 in an emergency).

There are a dozen pharmacies (*ljekarne*) spread around Dubrovnik, with no fewer than three on Stradun alone. Opening hours are usually 08.00–20.00, Monday to Friday, and 08.00–14.00 on Saturdays. Outside normal hours the two pharmacies below alternate as the duty pharmacy.

Ljekarna Kod Zvonika Stradun; tel: 321 133.
Ljekarna Gruž Gružka abala; tel: 418 990. On the main port, just up from the Hotel Petka.

Local Transport

You're most likely to arrive either at Čilipi airport or the Gruž ferry terminal, so transfers from these to and from the old town are covered first in this section, followed by local buses, taxis, ferries, long-distance buses, driving and finally cycling.

AIRPORT TRANSFER

The newly rebuilt Čilipi airport is about 20km/half an hour south of town, and there's an airport shuttle which coincides with arriving Croatia Airlines flights. It returns to the airport from the Dubrovnik bus station an hour and a half before Croatia Airlines departures, and costs 25 kuna. If you're flying with anyone other than Croatia Airlines, then you'll need to take a taxi, which costs around 220 kuna if the meter's on, or 200 kuna cash in hand – if the meter's off make sure you've agreed and understood the fare with the driver before you set off.

PORT TRANSFER

Most shipping – barring a few fishing vessels and the taxi boats to Lokrum and Cavtat – comes in at the port of Gruž, which is about 2.5km northwest of the old town. Sadly the tram, which used to run from Gruž harbour to the Pile gate, has long gone. Local buses #1A, #1B and #3 however run from Gruž direct to Pile via the bus station about every half-hour.

There's a direct bus to the Ploče gate, too, in the shape of the #8, which also runs about half-hourly – this is the one you want if you're staying at any of the Ploče hotels. The only trick to remember is that if you're catching the #1A or #3 you need to be heading down the quay, southwards, whereas if you're catching the #8 you need to go up the quay, northwards – the bus then does a loop round the one-way system, taking about 20 minutes to get to Ploče, and then goes round behind the city walls to Pile.

If you've just missed a bus then it's probably worth walking as far as the bus station – only about 500m south of the port – where you can catch a #1A, #1B, #3 or #6 to Pile.

LOCAL BUSES

Flat fare *Libertas* buses cover the whole of Dubrovnik and most run from 05.00 to midnight. Tickets can be bought in advance from newspaper kiosks at 8 kuna apiece, or on the bus for 10 kuna – and you'll be expected to have the right money.

The main bus routes used by visitors are:

#1A and #1B	from Pile to the bus station and on to Gruž; about every half-hour.
#3	from Pile to Gruž; about once an hour.
#4	from Pile to Lapad, passing many of the main hotels and terminating at the newly reopened Dubrovnik Palace; two to three times an hour.

#5	from Pile to the Lapad post office and on to the Hotel Neptun on Babin Kuk; about once an hour. The return route goes round the one-way system, arriving at the Ploče gate and then going round behind the old town walls to Pile.
#6	from Pile to the bus station, then up to the Lapad post office, terminating at the Dubrovnik President Hotel on Babin Kuk; about four times an hour.
#7B	from Gruž to the bus station and then up towards Lapad, passing the Hotel Bellevue and the Lapad post office before terminating at the Dubrovnik President Hotel on Babin Kuk; about once an hour.
#8	from Pile to the bus station, then on to Gruž where it goes into a one-way system which ends by coming down the hill past the Ploče hotels to the Ploče gate, and round behind the old town walls to Pile; two to three times an hour, but less frequently at weekends.
#9	from the bus station up to the Lapad post office and on to the hospital before taking a shorter return route to the bus station; about once an hour.
#10	from the bus station to Cavtat; about once an hour. The fare to Cavtat is 12 kuna and you pay on the bus.

TAXIS

Notwithstanding the excellent local buses, Dubrovnik has plenty of taxis, too. There are five taxi stands, at Pile (tel: 424 343), Ploče (tel: 423 164), Gruž (tel: 418 112), the bus station (tel: 357 044) and Lapad (on Kralja Tomislava, just before the Lapad post office; tel: 435 715). You can also call taxis from any of the main hotels.

You should check the meter's switched on when you set off – unless you've pre-negotiated a fare. How much you finally pay will depend largely on the state of Dubrovnik's traffic, which can get quite nastily snarled up, especially in the rush hour and throughout the summer. The meter should start at 25 kuna, and notch up 8 kuna per kilometre and 80 kuna per hour of waiting time (2004 prices). Typically you might pay 50 kuna from Gruž to Pile, or 70 kuna from Pile to one of the Lapad hotels.

A personal recommendation for excursions or even just for shorter trips, is to give the personable Nikša Prizmić a call on his mobile (tel: 091 531 0022) – he has more (and more extraordinary) tales to tell than you'd believe, coupled with a fine sense of humour. Hopefully by the time you read this he will also have a new taxi.

FERRIES AND TAXI BOATS

If you're visiting any of the islands near Dubrovnik you'll need to find your way on to one of the local ferries or taxi boats.

Taxi boats make the ten-minute crossing to Lokrum from Dubrovnik's old port every half-hour in summer, and you'll expect to pay about 15 kuna each way. Out of season just wander down to the port and ask around – there's always someone willing to take you out, and come and collect you for the return trip when you're ready (make sure you and the ferryman have agreed on a time). For a private service like this you need to negotiate the fare in advance – 50 to 100 kuna should get you there and back.

The old port

Regular boats also go to and from Cavtat from the old port in season. Although it's slower and (at around 20 kuna one-way) more expensive than the bus, it's a lovely way to travel, and takes you from the heart of Dubrovnik to the heart of Cavtat.

All other ferries leave from the main quay on Gruž harbour, with most being operated by Jadrolinija (www.jadrolinija.hr), the national ferry company, .

Jadrolinija runs foot-passenger ferries to the Elaphite islands two to four times a day, doing a loop from Dubrovnik to Koločep to Lopud to Šipan and back again – make sure you know the return ferry times before you set off. There's a daily (foot-passenger and car) ferry to Mljet, too, though as this arrives in Mljet in the afternoon and returns in the morning it does mean an overnight stopover. In summer, there's also a fast catamaran, which goes to Mljet in the morning and returns in the afternoon, making day trips perfectly feasible.

There are also huge Jadrolinija liners which ply the whole length of the coast from Pula and Rijeka to Split and Dubrovnik, once a day in each direction.

Ferries and taxi boats

If you're on foot you generally don't need to book ahead, though you do need to buy your tickets in advance as you can't get on the ferries without one. The Jadrolinija office is on the quay at Gruž, next door to the tourist-office kiosk, while tickets for the Mljet catamaran can be bought from Atlantagent, set back from the quayside amongst a row of travel agencies.

Fares are very reasonable indeed – in the summer of 2004 it cost passengers a paltry 11 kuna one-way to Koločep. The Jadrolinija fare to Mljet was only 18 kuna; with even the fast catamaran there costing just 25 kuna. Even the coastal liner which goes all the way to Rijeka only costs around 200 kuna for the 22-hour journey (though two or three times more if you want a cabin).

LONG-DISTANCE BUSES

It's unlikely that you'll be taking long-distance buses if you're reading this guide, but just in case you are, this section might be useful. It's also worth knowing that the bus station has Dubrovnik's only left-luggage facility, open from 04.30 to 21.00 daily.

Long-distance buses from Dubrovnik serve destinations all over the country and even venture abroad. There are eight buses a day to Zagreb, five to Rijeka, and nearly 20 to Split, as well as one apiece to Ljubljana (Slovenia), Sarajevo (Bosnia), Trieste (Italy) and Ulcinj (Montenegro), and two a week to Frankfurt and Munich. If you take the daily bus to Korčula, the fare includes the ferry crossing.

Hourly speeds on long-distance routes come in at about 45km/h, fares cost around 30–40 kuna per 100km, and you should buy your ticket as far ahead as you can.

Long-distance buses stop every two hours or so for a break, and the driver shouts out the duration of this above the din: *pet, deset, petnaest* and *dvadeset minuta* are the commonest break lengths (5, 10, 15, 20 min). These invariably occur where you can grab a quick drink/snack/meal. Watch the driver and you won't go far wrong, but be warned that the bus will go without you if you make a mistake.

DRIVING

If you're driving locally, be warned that parking in Dubrovnik can be both a problem and expensive. Hotel car parks tend to be over-flowing, while street parking, especially in summer, is a non-starter. There are two main car parks for the old town, one at the Pile gate (10 kuna an hour) and the other alongside the north wall (5 kuna an hour), though both fill up fast. There's also a larger car park at Gruž harbour (5 kuna an hour), which offers a long-term rate of 25 kuna a day.

If you park illegally you can definitely expect your car to be towed away by the ruthlessly efficient 'Sanitat Dubrovnik' tow-away service. The number to call when this happens is 331 016, 24 hours a day, and the pound, where your car will have been taken, is on Lichtensteineov put, in Lapad. The nearest bus route is the #9; take it to the terminus (the hospital) and walk round to the left to find the top end of Lichtensteineov put.

Driving

CYCLING

It's extremely unlikely (unless you're Dervla Murphy; see page 231) that you will have cycled here, but you may have considered bringing your bike with you on the plane. If so – and I'm saying this as a keen cyclist – think again. Croatia in general isn't really geared up for cyclists, and traffic – especially on the coast road – is downright dangerous. Cycling on the island of Mljet, however, is a real delight – but you can rent bikes when you get there.

HITCHHIKING

With public transport available and affordable this is definitely not recommended. Tourists are unlikely to pick you up and locals tend only to be travelling very short distances.

Accommodation

5

Note: Prices in this chapter are given in euros, as this is the currency used in pre-negotiations, reservations and official accommodation quotations – although your final bill will be in kuna. Prices were correct as of summer 2004.

Dubrovnik's long been popular with visitors, with the first proper accommodation for them opening in 1347, and private rooms coming on-stream in the second half of the 14th century. The Grand Hotel Imperial, with 70 rooms just up from the Pile gate, opened for business in 1897, but shut its doors again with the war in 1991. At the time of writing renovations were nearly complete and it should be reopening in 2005, as the Hilton Imperial.

During the siege of Dubrovnik (see page 24) the city lost around half of its total hotel stock, with damage being caused first by bombs and then by refugees flooding in afterwards. Indeed, if tourist numbers in 2003 were still a third below their 1990 levels, that's partly because of an accommodation shortage. The scene now, however, is improving fast, with most of the affected hotels restored and reopened. A dramatic exception is the Grand Libertas, in the Boninovo area of Lapad, which is a vast gutted shell – as you can see from the bus on the way up from Pile. In 2004, it was bought by Rixos Hotels, a Turkish chain, and will no doubt be renovated in the fullness of time.

Your main accommodation options in Dubrovnik are hotels or private rooms – of which there is a plentiful and growing supply. There's also a youth hostel and a solitary campsite (see page 112). Private rooms offer the best value for money, but if you're in the mood to splash out there's certainly plenty of choice at the top end of the market too.

Hotel accommodation fills up fast in summer, so it's definitely recommended that you reserve well ahead of time, and confirm by fax (web reservations have a habit of going missing). Private rooms can be booked on the fly, though those in the best locations fill up well in advance.

HOTELS

Croatian hotels are classified by the standard international star system, though at the lower end (which mostly means three star, in Dubrovnik) they don't represent exceptional value for money, especially when compared with the better private rooms. Also, bear in mind that while a view of the sea and a balcony are certainly desirable, you can get considerably cheaper rates if you're willing to forgo either – or indeed both – when there's a choice.

Breakfast is invariably included in room prices, and ranges from rolls, butter and jam to a full buffet, with a strong correlation between the quality of the food and the number of stars. You can save money by opting for half or full board – the supplement is usually under €20 per person per day – but bear in mind you'll also be condemning yourself to eating your meals in the hotel, rather than enjoying the old town. On the other hand, package hotels in particular will insist on half board, especially during high summer.

In terms of location, Dubrovnik has just two hotels in the old town; the rest are distributed around the smart suburb of Ploče just south of the old town, on the Lapad and Babin Kuk peninsulas, a few kilometres away, and in the port area of Gruž.

In the old town

Until recently, accommodation in the old town itself was limited to a handful of private rooms, but in 2003 two boutique hotels opened up for business. Bear in mind if you stay here that it can be stifling hot in summer, and views will be minimal – but on the other hand there's atmosphere in spades to be had from being inside the old walls.

Pučić Palace ★★★★★ Od Puča 1; tel: 326 200; fax: 326 323; www.thepucicpalace.com
Fabulously located on the corner of Gundulićeva poljana, the heart of the action in the old city, the Pučić Palace consists of just 19 rooms in a noble's luxuriously refurbished home. You could argue that the rooms – and particularly the bathrooms – have been over-restored, but you certainly couldn't complain about a lack of opulence. My favourite is the Ivan Gundulić room – though it's not the quietest, as it overlooks the square, which hosts both the early-morning market and the late-night revelry spilling out from the back door of the Troubadur (see page 128). As you'd expect it's not cheap – doubles go for €265 in winter and €465 in season, while a suite will set you back a rather dizzying €950 a night during the festival.

Hotel Stari Grad ★★★ Od Sigurate 4; tel: 321 373; fax: 321 256; www.hotelstarigrad.com
The newest hotel in the old town is the Stari Grad (meaning 'old town'), situated between
Stradun and Prijeko, only a couple of alleys in from the Pile gate. It's a tiny establishment,
with just eight rooms (four doubles, four singles) in an ancient renovated house. Old stone,
flagged floors and tasteful furniture don't quite over-ride the vague sense of unwelcome –
or perhaps that was just the day I was there. You won't have any kind of view from your
room (Od Sigurate is a narrow alley), but there is a fifth-floor terrace, with wicker furniture
and fine views across the rooftops, where you can breakfast in summer. Doubles go for
€132, singles for €91, year-round.

Ploče

If you can afford it, there's a lot to be said for staying in Ploče. The hotels overlook
the sea and the island of Lokrum and have *that* view of Dubrovnik's old town
walls and port. Seen in the light of early morning or late evening, it's a prospect
to die for.

Hotel Excelsior ★★★★★ Frana Supila 12; tel: 353 353; fax: 414 214; www.hotel-excelsior.hr
Just five minutes' walk uphill from the Ploče gate, the Excelsior consists of a stone 1920s
building and a largish glass and concrete annexe, for a total of nearly 200 rooms. It's
unashamedly luxurious, with a private beach, a fitness centre, a great big indoor swimming
pool with two Jacuzzis, and wonderful terraces where you can sip cocktails and admire the
views. The main restaurant, the Zagreb – which also serves as the breakfast room – is a bit

too big for comfort, but the Taverna Rustica, set apart from the hotel up its own private path, has great atmosphere and good regional cuisine.

Doubles with those incredible views go for €169 in winter, rising to €269 in summer; while for €319 you get a double with a balcony in summer (well worth the extra money). If you really want to splash out, try one of the lavish suites, which come in at €339 in winter and €589 in summer (the St Jacques suite, room 231a, has magnificent views of the old town through mirrored glass in the bathroom – as well as from the generous balcony).

The Excelsior offers great city breaks for €289 per person in winter and €329 in summer, comprising three nights in a room with a sea view, a dinner at the Taverna Rustica and airport transfers.

Hotel Villa Orsula ★★★★★ Frana Supila 14; tel: 440 555; fax: 432 524; www.hoteli-argentina.hr
Just 150m up the road from the Excelsior is the lovely Villa Orsula, under the same management (and connected to) the Grand Villa Argentina next door. The beautifully restored 1920s villa is somewhat dwarfed by the two big hotels on either side of it, but the rooms – and there are only a dozen – are delightful. All facilities are shared with the Argentina (see below). Double rooms with a sea view go for €210 in winter and €270 in summer; for an extra €20 you can get a (minuscule, but very attractive) stone balcony as well.

Hotel Grand Villa Argentina ★★★★★ Frana Supila 14; tel: 440 555; fax: 432 524; www.hoteli-argentina.hr

Hotels

In a very similar mould to the Excelsior, the Atlas-owned Argentina consists of a 1920s stone-built hotel with a modern annexe grafted on. It was entirely renovated in 2002, and offers everything you'd expect from a five-star hotel, including a small swimming pool and fitness centre. There are lovely gardens running down to the sea, and almost 2km of private beach. It's also well worth trying the Caravelle restaurant which specialises in Croatian cuisine. Double rooms with sea views come in at €207 in winter and €262 in summer; as at the Orsula, above, an extra €20 a night will get you a balcony, though they're considerably more spacious here.

Further up the hill from the Argentina is the **Villa Scheherazade**, which is now also owned by Atlas. Plans are to restore the Moorish-looking palace and convert it into a further luxury wing of the hotel. It certainly has plenty of atmosphere – it was formerly one of Tito's many residences, where (according to my trusty 1967 guide) the Marshal 'entertained Anthony Eden and many other world political figures.'

Villa Dubrovnik ★★★ Vlaha Bukovaca 6; tel: 422 933; fax: 423 465; www.villa-dubrovnik.hr Another 600m along the coast beyond the Villa Argentina (turn off the main road just after the Villa Scheherazade) is the Villa Dubrovnik. Walk down about 60 steps to get to reception, and you'll find the rest of the hotel is below this in terraces, dropping down to the rocky shoreline. The public areas are tastefully modern, light and airy, with white linen furnishings and rattan furniture, and the dining room and bar (and all the rooms) have gorgeous views back to the old town.

In general the amenities are excellent (all 40 rooms have sea views and balconies), and if it's considerably less formal and stuffy than the five-star hotels, it's no less pricey, in spite of the three-star rating. It has no swimming pool, but does have its own rocky beaches and a boat to take you into the old town, as well as a lovely outdoor area called the Bistro Giardino which is a perfect place for a pre-dinner drink. Double rooms go from €180 in winter to €264 in summer, while suites come in at €260 winter and €420 in summer.

Lapad, Babin Kuk and Gruž

Most of Dubrovnik's accommodation is spread out around the Lapad and Babin Kuk peninsulas, and mainly caters to package tours. It has the advantage of being away from the bustle, and most of the hotels have access to a beach, but you may find yourself further away from the old town than you wish to be. That said, it's only a matter of 5km from the furthest point on Lapad to the old town, and there are regular buses (see page 88). By taxi you're looking at a 10–20-minute ride, depending on the hotel location and traffic density.

Hotel Dubrovnik Palace ★★★★ Masarykov put 20; tel: 437 288; fax: 437 285; www.dubrovnikpalace.hr
Situated right at the end of the Lapad headland, Dubrovnik's biggest hotel finally reopened in 2004 after years of restoration and rebuilding which cost an estimated €37 million. The ten-floor, 320-room, 30,000m² complex boasts three outdoor swimming pools, rocky beaches and a diving centre, along with two indoor pools, two restaurants, 11 bars and a jazz club – as well as Dubrovnik's only presidential suite. Every room has a balcony and a sea view, and

behind the hotel are lovely paths up into the woods leading to stone belvederes with views out to sea. Double rooms go from €160 in winter to €250 in peak season.

Hotel Dubrovnik President ★★★★ Iva Dulčića 39; tel: 441 100; fax: 435 600; www.babinkuk.com

In a similar vein to the Dubrovnik Palace (though without the presidential suite, ironically) is the Dubrovnik President, which dominates the Babin Kuk headland – although it's smaller than its Lapad neighbour, with seven floors and 165 rooms. All rooms have a balcony and a view out across the sea to the Elaphite islands, and there's a fairly large beach area. It's unashamed upmarket package-tour territory, but the location is excellent and the atmosphere cheerful. Prices range from €128 for a double in winter to €238 for the same room in summer. The hotel is the flagship of the Babin Kuk group, which comprises three more hotels in the complex as well as Dubrovnik's only campsite.

Hotel Argosy ★★★ Iva Dulčića 41; tel: 446 100; fax: 435 578; www.babinkuk.com

Behind the President is the Argosy, a 300-room hotel which is a step down in both facilities and price, though it still has access to the beach and tennis courts etc, and boasts a decent-sized outdoor swimming pool. Winter rates for sea-view doubles come in at €80 per night rising to €160 in peak season.

Hotel Minčeta ★★★ Iva Dulčića 18; tel: 447 100; fax: 447 603; www.babinkuk.com

Further into the Babin Kuk headland, and facing the islet of Daksa, is the Minčeta. The sprawling four-storey building houses some 300 rooms, and is within reach of one of Dubrovnik's most popular beaches, the Copacabana, where you can indulge your taste for 'water polo, water skiing, scuba diving, wind surfing, and banana rides' … it says here. Double rooms with a sea view go for €54 in winter and €128 in summer.

Hotel Tirena ★★★ Iva Dulčića 22; tel: 445 100; fax: 445 602; www.babinkuk.com
Last of the four hotels in the complex is the Tirena, which is located between the Argosy and the Minčeta, and therefore also within reach of Copacabana beach, although only 28 of the Tirena's 190 rooms offer sea views. Its main advantage over the others is in being attached to the little local shopping centre. Double rooms with balconies go for €56 in winter and €116 in summer.

Hotel Neptun ★★★ Kardinala Stepinca 31; tel: 440 100; fax: 440 200; www.hotel-neptun.hr
In a great location on Babin Kuk, facing south and with rocky beaches and a couple of nice swimming pools, is the ten-storey Hotel Neptun. Its 150 rooms are bright and airy and most have sea views, with prices for doubles ranging from €76 in winter to €128 in summer.

Hotel Kompas ★★★ Šetalište Kralja Zvonimira 56; tel: 352 000; fax: 435 877; www.hotel-kompas.hr
Right down by the attractive Uvala Bay beach, which marks the meeting point of the Lapad and Babin Kuk peninsulas, is the Kompas. Its 115 rooms mostly have sea views, and it has its own indoor pool, but the hotel has seen better days. Fortunately it's now under the same

Hotels

management as the Excelsior and Dubrovnik Palace hotels, and plans are to upgrade it to four star over the next couple of years. Double rooms presently go for €74 in winter and €140 in high season.

Hotel Villa Wolff ★★★★ Nika I Meda Pučića 1; tel/fax: 435 353; www.villa-wolff.hr
Right next door to the Kompas is the Hotel Villa Wolff, which only opened in 2003. You wouldn't know it walking up the short flight of steep steps from the coastal path (next door to the Casa Bar), but above you is a charming little boutique hotel, with just half a dozen rooms (three doubles; one junior suite, two suites with balconies and sea views). It has its own terrace and Mediterranean garden, complete with rosemary bushes, palms, cypresses and ancient olive trees, with a great view across the bay. Doubles go for €160 in winter and €230 in summer, while the suites come in at €330 a night.

Hotel Komodor ★★★ Masarykov put 5; tel: 437 301; fax: 437 401; www.hotelimaestreal.com
Across the bay from the Kompas, and firmly back on Lapad, is one of the peninsula's oldest hotels, the Komodor – the first in a line of five establishments along Masarykov put run by the Maestral hotel chain. The Komodor was refurbished in 1999, and has 64 rooms and an outdoor swimming pool. Rates for a double room with a sea view and a balcony run from €78 in winter to €158 in summer.

Hotel Adriatic ★★ Masarykov put 9; tel: 437 302; fax: 437 402; www.hotelimaestreal.com
Just up the road is one of Dubrovnik's last-remaining two-star hotels, the Adriatic. With 158

rooms priced at €58 for a sea-view double in winter and €108 in summer, and a beach just across the street, it's something of a bargain – and almost invariably fully booked.

Hotel Uvala ★★★★ Masarykov put 6; tel: 433 580; fax: 433 590; www.hotelimaestreal.com
Almost next door (notwithstanding the street number) is the newest addition to the group, the brand new Uvala 'health and wellness centre', which promises to pamper the guests in its 51 rooms, most of which have sea views. Those doubles start at €128 a night in winter, rising to €218 in summer.

Hotel Vis ★★★ Masarykov put 4; tel: 437 303; fax: 437 403; www.hotelimaestreal.com
Next up, but over on the seaward side of the street, is the Hotel Vis, whose main attraction is being right on its own decent-sized beach. The hotel has 136 rooms, and sea-view doubles go for €68 a night in winter and €138 a night in summer – like the Adriatic, it's very often full up.

Hotel Splendid ★★ Masarykov put 10; tel: 437 304; fax: 437 404; www.hotelimaestreal.com
Last of the bunch is the Splendid, which like the Vis is right on the beach. It has 59 rooms, all with sea views and balconies, with doubles going for €88 in winter and €198 in summer.

Grand Hotel Park ★★★ Šetalište Kralja Zvonimira 39; tel: 434 444; fax: 434 885; www.grandhotel-park.hr
Situated between the Kompas and the Komodor, and set back from the Uvala beach, is the boxy Grand Hotel Park. Don't be fooled by the name; it has pretty good indoor and outdoor

sea-water swimming pools, but it's seriously in need of refurbishment (does the furniture have to be inventoried in every room?), making the sea-view double-room price tag (apparently year-round, but you can negotiate in winter) of €125 look pretty steep. It's not doing itself any favours, either, by employing one of the rudest receptionists I've ever encountered.

Hotel Dubrovnik ★★★ Šetalište Kralja Zvonimira bb; tel: 435 030; fax: 435 999; www.hoteldubrovnik.hr
Nicer by far is the Hotel Dubrovnik (not to be confused with the Villa Dubrovnik, the Dubrovnik Palace or the Dubrovnik President), all of 100m away, which may have neither indoor nor outdoor pools, but does have 15 clean, well-appointed rooms at very reasonable rates, and a welcoming staff. Double rooms go for €84 per night in winter and €110 in summer.

Hotel Sumratin ★★ Šetalište Kralja Zvonimira 31; tel: 436 333; fax: 436 006; no website
Further inland still is the 40-room Sumratin, which has neither sea views nor a swimming pool, but has the virtue of being simple, clean and great value for money, with doubles at €50 a night in winter and €81 a night in summer – making it one of Dubrovnik's most affordable hotels.

Hotel Zagreb ★★ Šetalište Kralja Zvonimira 27; tel: 436 146; fax: 436 006; no website
Almost next door to the Sumratin – and under the same management – is one of my favourite hotels in Dubrovnik, the Zagreb. It's only two star, but it offers 22 clean doubles at

knock-down prices in a lovely refurbished old building. Double rooms cost €53 in winter and €87 in summer.

Hotel Lapad ★★★ Lapadska obala 37; tel: 432 922; fax: 424 782; www.hotel-lapad.hr
Situated down on the shore of Babin Kuk, facing Gruž harbour, is the Lapad, which is based around a renovated old building with a modern annexe, and now comprises nearly 200 rooms. There's a small swimming pool, and the nearest beach is about 600m up the shore. Sea-view (port-view) doubles go for €74 in winter and €124 in summer – and if you're here in July or August, make sure you ask for one of the rooms with AC.

Hotel Petka ★★★ Obala Stjepana Radića 38; tel: 410 500; fax: 410 127; www.croatia-vacation.com
Situated right next to the main ferry-landing in Gruž (more or less directly across the water from the Hotel Lapad, above), the Petka features 104 rooms, all air conditioned, 64 of which have balconies giving on to the picturesque port. It's nothing fancy, but gives easy access to the islands, and is only a short bus ride away from the old town. And the prices are excellent value by Dubrovnik standards – doubles with sea views and balconies go for €70 in winter and €92 in summer.

Hotel Lero ★★★ Iva Vojnovića 14; tel: 341 333; fax: 332 133; www.hotel-lero.hr
Although entirely renovated in 1998, the Lero still retains something of its 1971 feel – and its

location on a busy main road may put some people off. But it's only a 15–20-minute walk from the Pile gate, on a bus route, 200m from the nearest beach, and half of the 150 rooms have sea views. At €52 for a double in winter and €96 for the same room in summer it's pretty good value – and the half-board supplement is a veritable snip at €5 per person per day.

Hotel Bellevue★★ Pera Čingrije 7; tel: 413 306; fax: 414 058; www.hotel-bellevue.hr
In a wonderful location just 10–15 minutes' walk up the hill from the Pile gate and benefiting from its own private beach, the cliff-top Bellevue is one of Dubrovnik's last great bargains. The rooms are pretty functional (hence the two-star billing) but many have their own balconies, and the prices are unbeatable for what you're getting – at €66 in winter and €110 in summer for doubles with sea views. The hotel has recently become part of the group that includes the Excelsior, the Dubrovnik Palace and the Kompas, and will in the fullness of time be upgraded to five star. If you're on a budget – as I so often have been in Dubrovnik – enjoy it while you can.

PRIVATE ROOMS/APARTMENTS

Dubrovnik has a huge supply of private rooms (*privatne sobe*) available, and for many independent travellers these represent their best accommodation option. Private rooms are the equivalent of B&Bs in the UK (though usually without breakfast), and are generally clean, comfortable and friendly. Their big advantage over hotels is their cost, with most private double rooms going for under €60 a night, even in summer.

The obvious way of finding a private room is through one of Dubrovnik's ubiquitous travel agencies (see page 76 for a selection), who will generally welcome your business. There are also a number of online resources if you want to book/look ahead – over a hundred properties are listed at each of www.dubrovnik-apartments.com and www.dubrovnik-online.com/english/private_accommodation.php, for example.

If you come in by ferry or bus, you're likely to be assailed on arrival by offers of private rooms. These may work out cheaper than anything you can get through travel agents, and unless the season's especially busy you can haggle – but check both the location and total price very carefully before accepting an offer.

You can also wing it, by knocking on doors where you see signs saying any of *sobe, zimmer, chambres, camere, rooms* or *privat* – but this can be a terrible waste of time, especially if you're only on a short break. (If you do decide to go this route, a good place to start looking is in Lapad, in the area around Ispod Petke.)

Private rooms are officially classified into categories, I, II and III. Category I rooms will be clean and functional, but you'll almost certainly be sharing a bathroom. In Category II you'll be bathing en suite and may even have a TV, while in Category III you'll find yourself very well looked after.

In terms of cost, the cheapest double rooms start at about €20 per night, out of season, but for anything in a good location in summer you should expect to pay €40 to €60 per night (bearing in mind that prices are usually quoted per person, not per room) – and for anything in Ploče or the old town itself prices go up to

€100 in season. If you're staying for under three nights a surcharge (of anything from 20–50%) is applicable. In theory, if you're travelling alone then you pay around 70% of the full price to stay in a double room, but in a seller's market you may well end up paying the full whack.

Private accommodation also includes apartments, which can be great value for families or small groups – but check how many beds have been crammed into each room before you agree to anything. More expensive apartments tend to be better-located rather than roomier.

Finally, with both private rooms and apartments don't be afraid to say no if you don't like the look of the place – staying somewhere which doesn't suit you can really spoil your holiday.

Of the places I've stayed recently, the outstanding recommendation has to go to the **Karmen apartments** (at Bandureva 1; tel: 323 433; mob: 091 332 4106; www.karmendu.tk; email: – the best way of reserving, for once – apartments@karmendu.tk). These are situated in an ancient stone building in a stunning location right on the old port. Run by Marc and Silva van Bloemen, there are four apartments. One and Two have a double bed and a separate single; Three has a double and a single in the same room, and Four is a small double. Of these my favourite is Apartment One, which has a stunning view of the old port and clocktower, across the city walls, though Apartment Two does have a charming little balcony. The rooms are spacious, comfortably and tastefully furnished, and come fully equipped with kitchen, satellite TV, CD player, etc. Living in the same building are Marc's parents,

Michael and Sheila van Bloemen, long-time activists and founders of the legendary Troubadour Club in London, which they ran in its heyday, from 1954 to 1972. The three apartments go for €60 a night in winter and €100 a night in summer, with a 20% surcharge for stays of under three nights. The double room is 30% cheaper.

Also highly recommended are the rooms run by **Kathy Ljubojević** and her husband Niko (at Put Petra Kresimira IV 33; tel: 423 412; email: info@bedandbreakfast-dubrovnik.com; www.bedandbreakfast-dubrovnik.com). The house is high up in Ploče with a staggering view down on to the old town and across to Lokrum (it's a short but steep ten-minute hike up from the Ploče gate – head up Ul Bosanka, right beside the Maesosto restaurant – or a five-minute walk down). There are four clean, tidy rooms which range from €35 to €60 in winter and €55 to €80 in summer; the front two have balconies and those stupendous views. You can also buy great gifts to take home here, too, as Niko is an expert maker of designer glassware (see page 138).

Finally, if you're on a tight budget, it's well worth contacting **Ivo Gugić** (Hvarska 46; tel: 417 354; mob: 091 517 0693; no website or email), who has three rooms just round the corner from the Pile gate, outside the city walls. They're decidedly functional, but at €15 per person in winter and €20 per person in summer, what would you expect?

YOUTH HOSTEL

Dubrovnik also has a youth hostel (Vinka Sagrestana 3; tel: 423 421; fax: 412 592; www.hfhs.hr). It's in a pretty good location, about 15 minutes uphill from the bus station, just off Bana Jelačića, and for single people on a budget it's as cheap as you'll find in Dubrovnik, at €12 to €16 per person. That said, as you can imagine it's very hard to secure one of the 80-odd places, especially in summer, and for two or more people travelling together private accommodation can be not only more convenient – no daytime lockout, for example – but also competitive on price and location.

CAMPING

Dubrovnik has one campsite, on the Babin Kuk peninsula (managed by the Babin Kuk complex), but unless you're absolutely desperate to get under canvas, I can't really recommend it as an accommodation option for a short break. Having said that, if you are coming here with your tent, the Auto-Camp Solitudo (Iva Dulčića 39; tel: 448 686; fax: 448 688; www.babinkuk.com) offers 166 pitches, newly refurbished bathrooms and laundry areas, and charges €7 to €10 per pitch, €3.20 to €5.40 per person and a one-off fee of €20 per reservation. It's also close to various beaches and within striking distance of Copacabana.

Finally, remember that freelance camping in Croatia is illegal. If you're caught you'll be subject to an immediate and fairly hefty fine.

Eating and Drinking

6

Dubrovnik has no shortage of eateries and drinking establishments, but before listing them it's worth taking a moment to look at what you might be eating and drinking while you're here.

FOOD AND DRINK
Food

The day starts for most of us with breakfast, though it practically doesn't exist as a meal *per se* in Dubrovnik. If you're in a hotel, then breakfast of some sort will invariably be included in the price – usually in the form of a self-service buffet, with the quality and variety of fare on offer closely correlating to the number of stars.

If you're in a private room you can rely on cafés and *slastičarnice* (cake shops) to sell you pastries and cakes for breakfast, and if you're outside the old town you may still find *burek*, a pastry filled with cheese (*sa sirom*), meat (*sa mesom*) and just occasionally spinach (*špinat*). *Burek* is cheap, filling and usually delicious – if occasionally too greasy for comfort – but a good deal harder to find than it was a decade or so ago.

Outside the old town you'll also find cheap restaurants and snack bars – often billed as *bife* (bar) or *roštilj* (grill bar) – serving up lunch or dinner of *čevapi or čevapčiči* (spiced meatballs or small sausages, usually served with spring onions and spicy green peppers), *pljeskavica* (a wad of minced meat often served in pitta bread

– the Croatian hamburger), or *ražnjiči* (kebab). Try any of these dishes with fiery *ajvar*, a sauce made from tomatoes, peppers and aubergines, with a dash of chilli.

Bakeries (*pekarnica*) sell a wide variety of breads (though occasionally only powdery white rolls and plain loaves) and sometimes offer ready-made sandwiches (*sendviči*) available with cheese (*sir*) or ham (*šunka*) fillings. Street markets (*tržnica*) will provide you with the usual fare for picnics etc, and you can ask for sandwiches to be made up to order at any deli-counter in a supermarket (*samospluga*) – just point at the type of bread you want filled, say '*sendvič*' and point at your choice of filling.

Pizzerias are the next step up the food chain, and represent great value for money. Pizza here is close to what you get in Italy, with a thin crust and a variety of toppings – including excellent chilli peppers. Pizzerias also tend to do good (and keenly priced) pasta dishes – though I've yet to eat pasta anywhere in Croatia that wasn't (by Italian standards, anyway) slightly overcooked.

Restaurants (*restoran, konoba or gostiona*) tend to focus on meat and/or fish dishes. Meat isn't especially exciting, tending towards pork and lamb chops and cutlets, pan-fried veal, or steak, but it's generally tasty enough. Fish for its part is ubiquitous and delicious – but can turn out to be surprisingly pricey. For most white fish you'll pay by the raw weight, and a decent-sized fish for two can come in at as much as 400 kuna on its own. Whitebait, blue fish (sardines, mackerel, etc) and squid are, on the other hand, great value.

Shellfish is especially popular in Dubrovnik, with steamed mussels on many menus and cockles appearing in pasta dishes and starters, and in winter (through to mid-May) you can get great oysters here (from Ston) priced at 5 to 10 kuna apiece. You may also see crab and lobster on the menu – but mind the price tag (and watch out for mis-translations; crayfish is often billed as lobster). Finally, you'll see plenty of *crni rižot* (literally black risotto) on offer; it's a pungent dish, made with squid ink, and though it's popular it's not to everyone's taste.

You'll also see lots of *pršut*, Croatia's answer to Italy's *prosciutto*, and pronounced (and produced) in almost exactly the same way. The air-dried ham is a Dalmatian speciality and practically melts in the mouth when sliced thinly enough – which sadly it isn't always.

Unless of course you're vegetarian, in which case *pršut*, like much else on the menu, is a non-starter – indeed it's a non-main and a non-dessert, too. Vegetarianism is no longer off the menu altogether, however, and even where restaurants don't offer specific vegetarian options, you can always get a cheese omelette (*omlet sa sirom*), a meat-free pasta dish, or a pizza, along with a range of salads.

Drink

The most important thing to know is that you *can* drink the water – all publicly supplied water in Dubrovnik is safe unless it explicitly says otherwise. The next piece of good news for drinkers is that alcohol is pretty inexpensive when compared with northern Europe, with a half-litre of draught **beer** (*pivo*) costing anything from 10–20 kuna, depending on the watering hole. Premium and foreign brands go for a little more, but Croatian beers suit most tastes.

Croatia makes lots of **wine** *(vino)*, and the quality – always drinkable – continues to improve. Almost the entire production is guzzled down domestically, so you're very unlikely to see it on your supermarket shelves at home. In shops you can pay anything from 20–100 kuna for a bottle, while in low- to mid-range pizzerias and restaurants a litre of the house red or white goes for 50–100 kuna, with bottled wines starting at around 80 kuna. Swankier establishments don't usually sell house wine, and you can easily find yourself spending upwards of 200 kuna a bottle. The nearest big wine-growing region to Dubrovnik is the Pelješac peninsula (home to a host of reds) and the island of Korčula (which produces excellent whites – including three of my personal favourites, Vrbnička, from Vrbnik, Grk, from Lumbarda and Pošip).

Spirits *(rakija)* are common, dangerous, and fairly cheap. In supermarkets you'll find brandies and other spirits at around 70–100 kuna a bottle, but you can also buy fiery and frequently excellent home-distilled spirits – especially *travarica*, a drink featuring a lot of alcohol and a few herbs – in the markets for anything from 50–100 kuna a bottle. The quality of spirits varies enormously and can't usually be determined from the label – price is a reasonable (but far from infallible) indicator.

Friendships, business deals and meetings are all cemented with *rakija*, and it's surprising how often you'll find yourself expected to down a fiery shot. If you don't drink at all, then it's not a bad idea to come up with a plausible reason for this (health is a reliable standby), as Croats tend to be suspicious of people who won't join in.

In marked contrast to the abundance of alcoholic choice, there are surprisingly few **soft drinks** available. You're basically limited to the usual mind-numbingly popular cola (but rarely the sugar-free variety), bottles of sweet fizzy orange and mineral water.

Coffee is as popular here as everywhere, and in cafés tends to be excellent – though what you'll be served with breakfast in the lower-end hotels can be frankly disgusting. **Tea** is most often of the fruit variety or comes in dodgy-looking bags which tend to work better with lemon than milk. Ordinary 'English' tea is known as black tea (*crni caj*), but don't expect to find anything you'll be able to stand a spoon in. Tea and coffee will cost anything from 5 to 15 kuna in a café, depending on the upmarketness (or otherwise) of the place.

RESTAURANTS

As you'd expect, Dubrovnik is brimming with places to eat, though with a few exceptions there's often surprisingly little to distinguish one place from another. Food in the old town tends universally towards grilled fish, meat and shellfish at the upper end of the spectrum, and pizza and pasta dishes in the mid-tier establishments.

At places marked as inexpensive in the (alphabetical) listings below expect to pay around 200 kuna for two, including wine; mid-range places will set you back 250–500 kuna for a couple; while at expensive restaurants two can easily pay 600 kuna and up – though there's nothing to stop you having a soup, a salad and a glass of wine at a ritzy place and coming away with change from 300 kuna for two.

Most restaurants catering to tourists are open from around 11.00 to 23.00, though some will close for a period during the afternoon – and in summer places will stay open until midnight or 01.00. Expect to pay a cover charge of around 5 to 10 kuna per person. Reservations are not normally expected (or accepted); places where reservations are recommended are marked in the listings below.

In the old town

Dubrovnik's busiest restaurant district is along Prijeko, the street running parallel to Stradun for its entire length. Unfortunately it's managed to get itself something of a bad reputation over the years, which hasn't been helped by the touts along Stradun trying to entice in passing trade. While there is no doubt good food to be had, there's a level of unscrupulousness here which probably comes from knowing the chances are you won't be coming back, and tales of poor-quality food and routine over-charging are legion. It's a pity, as the location is perfect and the atmosphere ought to be first-rate. The one exception to the Prijeko rule seems to be Rozarij, right at the eastern end of the street.

Baracuda I Nikole Božidarevićeva 10 [1 B3]
One of the smallest yet cheeriest restaurants in town, serving up tasty pizzas and very little else (there really isn't room). Situated just off Od Puča, near the Serbian Orthodox church. It has a slightly larger sister-establishment on Lapad (see page 123). Inexpensive.

Eating and drinking

Domino Od Domina 3; tel: 323 103 [1 B3]
At the top end of Od Domina, not far from the inside of the sea wall, Domino prides itself on its great steaks, but also has decent fish and seafood specialities, including a particularly good black (squid) risotto. The outside terrace is enduringly popular. Check out its sister-restaurant, Bistro Riva, on Lapad (see below). Mid-range.

Jadran Paska Milečevića 1 [1 A2]
The Jadran has a perfect location inside the old cloisters of the former Convent of St Clare (go through the alley to the right just after you come through the Pile gate, past a sports shop on the right and a souvenir shop on the left). Dating originally from the 13th century, the convent became the republic's orphanage in 1432, and an open-air cinema after World War II. The gorgeous setting is a triumph over the somewhat average fare, but it's a lovely place to sit and while away an hour or two – especially if it's windy, as it's a well-sheltered spot. Inexpensive to mid-range.

Kamenica Gundulićeva poljana 8 [1 C3]
Kamenica – literally small stone, but here meaning oyster – is a great place in a great location. It specialises in seafood, and in particular oysters, which in 2004 went for a very reasonable 7 kuna a pop. The menu is short but excellent, with the *frittura* (whitebait) and the squid particularly good, and the house wine an all-too affordable 56 kuna a litre. Highly recommended, so catch it while you can – there were rumblings in 2004 about lease renewals and possible closure. Inexpensive.

Labirint Svetog Dominika 2; tel: 322 222 [1 D3]

After more than a decade of renovation, the upmarket Labirint is finally open again. Set into the city walls near the Dominican Monastery, it offers a top-notch restaurant as well as various bars, terraces and a discreet nightclub. The fish soup – which goes for 10–20 kuna in most places – costs 45 kuna here (but is worth it), while pasta dishes come in at around 80 kuna. Mussels are expensive at 140 kuna, with mouth-watering scallops a much better deal at 180 kuna. Expect meat dishes to cost 150 to 200 kuna and wine to set you back around 200 kuna or more a bottle. Expensive; booking essential in season and on weekends.

Lokanda Peskarija Na Ponti [1 D3]

Absolutely my favourite place in Dubrovnik out of season, even if it does have one of the world's shortest menus – or perhaps because of it. Situated right on the old port, the establishment is tiny, with a bar downstairs and a handful of tables upstairs, though in fine weather it quickly spreads out across the quayside. The fried squid here is unrivalled, and the oysters – at 5 kuna apiece – are not just the cheapest but amongst the best in town. Ask for the excellent fish pâté, which isn't on the foreign-language menus, or the delicious marinated anchovy fillets. Inexpensive.

Mea Culpa Za Rokom 3 [1 A3/B3]

Owned by the same people as Lokanda Peskarija (see above), Mea Culpa is an unpretentious place at the other end of town, serving up terrific pizza and not a whole lot else (not even salad, when I was in town). Tables spill out on to the street, and it's a popular place with locals and visitors alike, with draught Guinness on tap. Inexpensive.

Poklisar Ribarnica 1 [1 D2]

Poklisar has a great location right on the old port, next to the fish market (*riba* means fish). It has a lovely terrace and serves up the usual range of fish dishes as you'd expect, as well as reasonable pizzas – though you could argue that you're paying as much for the setting as for the food here. Claims to be open from 07.00 to midnight – and in high season that may well be true. Inexpensive (pizza)/mid-range (fish).

Proto Široka 1; tel: 323 324 [1 B2]

Proto is one of Dubrovnik's most famous landmarks, and makes a big deal about having been in business since 1886 and having had Edward VIII and Wallis Simpson to dinner in the 1930s. But in spite of the hype there's a lot to be said for both the fish and meat dishes here, which are probably as good as anywhere in town – and the upstairs terrace is always packed in summer. Expensive; worth reserving.

Rozarij Zlatarska 4 [1 D2]

On the corner of Prijeko but with an address on Zlatarska, Rozarij breaks the Prijeko mould (see the introductory section, above), serving up unpretentious local Croatian fare in a nice setting near the Dominican Monastery. Inexpensive to mid-range.

Toni Nikole Božidarevićeva 14 [1 B2]

Just a couple of doors up from the Baracuda 1 (see above) is Spaghetteria Toni, which serves up just about the best pasta in town. Check out the tasty – and vast – home-made lasagne or the various pasta dishes with seafood sauces. It's cheerful, informal and highly popular with locals – last time I ate there the director of the modern art gallery was having dinner with friends at the next table.

Snack bars

If you're on a tight budget – or just don't fancy sitting down for a meal – there is a variety of snack bars and sandwich joints in town. Two of the best are near each other, towards the Pile end of Stradun. The first is the **Buffet Škola** [1 B2], which is on Antuninska, on the left-hand side heading up towards Prijeko. Here you can get terrific home-made sandwiches filled with cheese or *pršut* for just 15 or 20 kuna. Across Stradun, in Široka, right by Proto (see previous page), is the **Fish Sandwich Bar** [1 B2], which sells wonderful … well, fish sandwiches. Fillings include fried fish or mussels and prices range from 15 to 25 kuna. Both places are open – broadly speaking – from about 10.00 to 14.00 and 18.00 to 21.00.

Ice-cream

Dubrovnik's also great for ice-cream. There are three main establishments in the old town. The best-located, right by Onofrio's fountain, is perhaps predictably the least good of the three. Somewhat better is the place down at the other end of

Stradun, on the right-hand side; but best of all is the **Dolce Vita** [1 B2], on Nalješkovićeva, one of the streets between Stradun and Prijeko, which serves quite the tastiest and freshest ice-cream (and frozen yoghurt) in town.

Outside the old town walls

Baracuda II Ispod Petke 16 [2 C3]

Up in the heart of Lapad you'll find Baracuda I's (see page 118) sister-restaurant, appropriately named Baracuda II. It serves up perfectly acceptable pizzas and has considerably more space inside than its old-town partner, as well as an open rooftop terrace, which is a great place to shoot (and indeed catch) the breeze on a summer evening. Inexpensive.

Bistro Riva Lapadska Obala 20 [2 D2]

Situated on Gruž harbour, but opposite the port (just before the Hotel Lapad), is the Bistro Riva. Simpler and less expensive than its sister restaurant, Domino, in the old town (see page 119), it serves up a wide range of tasty dishes including good pizzas. The only pity is that the courtyard is closed in, blocking off what would be great views across the water. Inexpensive.

Casa Nika i Meda Pučića 1 [2 B3]

Billed as 'Bar and Ristorante', Casa has a great location right on the waterfront at Uvala Bay, just where the Babin Kuk and Lapad peninsulas meet. It's right under the Hotel Villa Wolff and next door to the Hotel Kompas, and marks the start of the path which goes clockwise

Restaurants

around Babin Kuk. It only actually serves food in summer, and then more of the snack variety than the full meal, but it's an excellent place to sit, with the light bouncing off the water. Inexpensive for food; mid-range for drinks.

El Toro Ivo Vojnovića 5 [2 E4/F4]
Just up the road from the Hotel Bellevue, with a nice leafy high-up terrace, you'll find the Café Pizzeria El Toro, which is cheap and cheerful and serves up reasonable pizzas at a good price. Inexpensive.

Levanat Nika i Meda Pučića 15; tel: 432 352 [2 A3]
With an unbeatable waterfront location on Babin Kuk, Levanat is secluded, upmarket, pricey, and altogether wonderful. It's easy to get to on foot by walking along the footpath which starts at Casa (see page 123) for about ten minutes, or from the Babin Kuk or Neptun hotels; otherwise you might want to consider getting a taxi, as it's quite a schlep from the old town. The menu focuses on excellent – and by Croatian standards – original fish dishes. You can also come here just for a drink. Expensive; reservations recommended (not least to check it's open).

Maesosto Put od Bosanke 4 [2 J4]
Well-known and popular restaurant just outside the Ploče gate with a view across to the old town harbour. The fare is the traditional grilled meat and fish, but the place is (in this author's opinion) somewhat over-rated. Mid-range.

Nautika Brsalje 3; tel: 442 573 [2 H4]

For years the ritziest place in town, the Atlas Club Nautika (to give its full name and let you know who owns it) trades heavily on having had Pope John Paul II to lunch on June 6 2003, though it's hard to imagine the aged pontiff scoffing his way through the five-course menu on display. These days I'd personally rather eat at Labirint or Levanat, though Nautika does have an excellent location, on the water, right outside the Pile gate, and a gorgeous pair of terraces, as well as smart dining rooms indoors. The food is excellent, as you'd expect for the price, and the service impeccable – but check your bill carefully as mistakes have been reported. Nautika also offers a 'Light Lunch' on the terrace outside, though I wasn't all that impressed. Expensive; reservations recommended.

Posat Uz Posat 1 [2 H4]

Well located outside the Pile gate (just up and to the right) is the Konoba Posat, which has a large and leafy terrace. It's as good a place as any for grilled meats. Inexpensive to mid-range.

Shanghai (or Šangaj, if you want the local spelling) Ante Starčićeva 25 [2 G4]

About 200m beyond the main tourist office, on the same side of the street, you'll find one of Dubrovnik's few Chinese restaurants. The food is everything you'd expect, though not comparable, sadly, to what you can get in the UK. Mid-range.

Taverna Rustica, Frana Supila 12; tel: 424 222 [2 K3/K4]

Part of the Hotel Excelsior, the Taverna Rustica is in a great location in Ploče, with views back to the old town. The food isn't half as rustic as the name implies, focusing on upmarket pasta dishes and local fish. Expensive; reservations recommended.

Tres Miyos Hvarska 6 [2 H4]

On the road running behind the old town (usually marked on maps as Iza Grada) you'll find a minute but friendly Mexican restaurant. It's a brave effort serving tortillas and chilli beans in a place where everyone's come for the fish, but it can make a pleasant change if you're here for a week. Inexpensive.

CAFÉS AND BARS

With great weather and lots of visitors, there's no shortage of places to drink in Dubrovnik, especially in the old town. Most restaurants with terraces will also be happy to serve you drinks between meals.

In the old town

Fashions change quickly in Dubrovnik, and today's groovy hangout can be tomorrow's leftover. Places also open up and shut down with dizzying speed – so please don't hesitate to write and let us know what's changed for the next edition.

Carpe Diem Kneza Damjana Jude 4 [1 E4]

Situated on the narrow street running down to the aquarium, and billing itself as an 'Art Caffe', Carpe Diem does a light breakfast in the morning and exotic cocktails in the evening. It's long, narrow, smartly decorated and popular late into the evening.

Cervantes Dropčeva 5 [1 C2]

Hard to know whether to put this under restaurants or bars, as Cervantes – located on one of the streets between Stradun and Prijeko – specialises in *tapas*. Their anchovies, in various formats, are excellent.

Festival Café Stradun [1 C2/D3]

Benefiting from a perfect location on Stradun, the Festival Café is especially popular through the day and in the early evenings, when it's a great place to see and be seen.

Gradska Kavana Pred Dvorom [1 D3]

In arguably the best location in town, next door to the Rector's Palace and opposite St Blaise's Church, the Gradska Kavana (literally 'town café') has a spacious interior and a raised terrace which is perfect for people-watching.

Hemingway Bar Pred Dvorom [1 D3]

Right opposite the Rector's Palace and next door to the cathedral is the new and popular Hemingway Bar, which attracts the cocktail-drinking set. It's impossible to imagine what Hemingway himself would have thought.

Irish Pub Od Polača 5 [1 C2/C3]

Just one street back from Stradun you'll find the Irish Pub, which although it's not a pub as you or I would know it, still serves a good range of beers and is popular with local students. Happy hour 15.00–18.00.

Cafés and bars

Ražanoda Od Puča [1 C3]
Next door to the Pučić Palace hotel and under the same management, Ražanoda is a swanky, upmarket wine bar with a good list of the best Croatian wines – and price tags to match.

Troubadur Bunićeva poljana [1 C3/C4]
Properly known as the Hard Jazz Café Troubadur, this is an excellent bar with a pub-like atmosphere and live music most evenings. The front door is on Bunićeva poljana and the back door is on Gundulićeva poljana. The establishment is owned by Marco, who was famous in the '60s and '70s as the bass player for the Dubrovački Troubaduri, who even made it once into the Eurovision song contest. Lots of musical memorabilia – showing Marco with a good deal more hair than he has today – covers the walls. If no-one else is playing then Marco himself will usually get up and do a turn on his double bass while a friend plays guitar. The tables outside are made from old sewing machines, which is an unusual touch.

Outside the old town walls
Needless to say, Dubrovnik has its own life beyond that aimed at tourists, and there are a couple of areas where this goes on, notably on Bana Jelačića, running up into Lapad, and on Ivo Vojnovića, in the heart of Lapad. A new scene has sprung up here in just the last couple of years, with a clutch of eight trendy new bars which are hugely popular with the locals and rarely visited by foreigners. Other than this, there are a handful of places worth noting:

Buža [1 D4]

Situated on the rocks outside the western (seaward) walls of the city, Buža is the place to come if you want to watch the sun go down. The only sounds are the sea and the gulls, and it's gloriously informal. The entrance is pretty well hidden and usually unsigned – go up behind the Jesuit church and out of the square on the opposite corner, and then turn right under the walls along Od Margarite. After a short while you come to a hole in the wall on your left (Buža means 'hole') which leads out on to the rocks – and there you are. Only open – you'll see why – when the weather's fine.

Casa Nika i Meda Pučića 1 [2 B3]

Casa has a great location right on the waterfront at Uvala Bay, and although the drinks are pricier than you might be used to (20 kuna for a beer), the situation alone makes it worth the visit – especially if you're about to set off on the lovely walk around Babin Kuk (see page 182).

Kavana Dubravka Brsalje [2 H4]

Occupying prime real estate right outside the Pile gate, opposite Nautika, the Kavana Dubravka has a lovely terrace set overlooking the little bay between the Bokar and Lovrijenac fortresses. Inside it's worth having a look at the photos on the walls of the old trams which used to ply their way up the hill from here. For 2 kuna you can use the toilets – which are a good deal more pleasant than the public ones over on the other side of the Pile gate.

Cafés and bars

7 Entertainment and Nightlife

Dubrovnik has a richly vibrant cultural scene, with its own symphony orchestra, theatre group and dance ensemble. Most performances take place during the season – broadly speaking from May to October – when there's usually something on every night. Most important of all is the annual Dubrovnik Summer Festival, which was inaugurated in 1950.

DUBROVNIK SUMMER FESTIVAL

Dubrovnik's Summer Festival is big, prestigious and serious, with every conceivable space in the old town – indoors and out – being turned into a performance stage. The 45-day festival kicks off on July 10 with the performers being given the keys to the city and closes on August 25 with a fabulous firework display.

During the festival you can find everything from opera and classical concerts to chamber music and soloists, while theatre performances tend to concentrate on Shakespeare and local boy Marin Držić (see page 150). A festival standard is the traditional performance of *Hamlet* in the Lovrijenac fortress, which is a wonderfully atmospheric setting for the play.

Tickets for the main events sell out well in advance, so if you're serious about attending check out the website (www.dubrovnik-festival.hr) or contact the organisers (tel: 323 400; fax: 323 365) as soon as the programme becomes available (usually in April) – and make sure you get your accommodation sorted out way ahead of time, too. If you haven't got tickets in advance there are usually places available for the lower-key performances on-site – you can buy these from the festival kiosks on Stradun and at the Pile gate.

MUSIC

Even outside the festival there are plenty of opportunities to listen to classical music, largely thanks to the tireless Dubrovnik Symphony Orchestra (www.dso.hr), which puts on an astonishing range of concerts, year-round.

The two most common venues – outside festival time – are the Revelin fortress, just outside the Ploče gate, and the Church of Our Saviour (Sveti Spas), just inside the Pile gate, where there are regular candlelit performances.

Tickets can be bought in advance from the DSO office at Ante Starčićeva 29 – about 300m up the street from the main tourist office, on the same side of the road. The office is set back from the street, where you'll also find an attractive little cocktail bar called La Bohème. Any tickets left over go on sale an hour before the performance, at the venue.

Other musical events tend to be less formally managed, with impromptu open-air rock and jazz performances happening at intervals throughout the summer – and of course there's live jazz most nights at the Troubadour (see page 128).

DANCE

Croatia has a tremendous tradition of folk dancing and Dubrovnik has one of the country's most famous troupes in the form of the 300-strong Linđo ensemble.

They're a regular mainstay of the festival, and also perform twice a week from May to October at the Lazareti, the old quarantine houses just up from the Ploče gate. It makes for an amazing and authentic spectacle. Linđo's office is at Marojice Kaboge 12, two streets back from Gundulićeva poljana.

On Sundays from May to October – except during the festival – there are also regular traditional dances and bands playing in front of St Blaise's Church. Also on Sundays the locals in the village of Čilipi, 25km south of Dubrovnik, put on a show after mass – and although it's become something of a tourist spectacle it's nonetheless an interesting thing to go and see if you have the time.

THEATRE

The theatre plays an important part of Dubrovnik life, and there are regular performances at the Marin Držić theatre, next door to the Rector's Palace. These are uniquely in Croatian, so unless your language skills are up to it you may prefer another cultural activity. Tickets are sold at the theatre itself – and by European standards they're inexpensive.

CINEMA

Dubrovnik's main cinema is right in the heart of the old town, next to the clocktower and the Gradska Kavana (see page 127). Fortunately for English-speakers, most of the films are subtitled rather than dubbed, straight from Hollywood. This makes going to the cinema easy enough, and tickets are cheap –

but you'll be lucky to find films made outside the US which you'll be able to understand without good language skills. I once sat through the full six hours of Bertolucci's *Novocento* in Italian, here, with Croatian subtitles; not something I'd necessarily recommend.

Dubrovnik also hosts an International Film Festival at the end of May.

NIGHTLIFE

Though there's plenty of late-evening café activity and drinking going on in the old town, actual nightlife is decidedly thin on the ground in Dubrovnik, with most places closing up by 01.00. In summer the last of the **Lazareti** [2 J4], out past the Ploče gate, features DJs and dancing, and probably the hippest music you'll find in the area – but Ibiza it ain't.

Just outside the Pile gate, at Brsalje 10, there's the **Latino Club Fuego** [2 H4], which is open from Thursday to Saturday nights from 22.00 to 04.00. It's one of the few places open that late and therefore popular with backpackers who've had a bit too much to drink. Otherwise there's **Labirint's** tiny nightclub in the town walls (part of the same establishment as the swanky restaurant, see page 120), which is open until 03.00; **Esperanza** [2 E3/F3], at Put Republike 30, just up from the bus station, which is popular with locals and sometimes puts on gigs; and the **Exodus** [2 A2] nightclub, out on Babin Kuk (and part of the Babin Kuk hotel complex) which offers the nearest you'll probably find to trance and techno. And that's your lot.

GAY AND LESBIAN

If the nightlife is thin on the ground, the gay and lesbian scene is non-existent. If anyone can recommend a gay or lesbian bar or club in Dubrovnik please don't hesitate to write and let me know – so we can remedy this lamentable lacuna.

BEACHES

The other way of entertaining yourself, of course, is with a trip to the beach. The nicest ones are out on the island of Lokrum, and it's well worth getting out there if you possibly can (see page 175) – it's also the nearest naturist beach to the old town.

If you simply fancy cooling off after a hot walk around the city walls, walk just round the corner at the old port and there's a swimming area off the rocks, by the jetty.

The city's main public beach, though, is the Banje beach, just outside the Ploče gate, facing the old port. It's recently been refurbished and you can now rent parasols and deckchairs here, and order yourself cocktails at the summer bar. In spite of being right next to the old port the water is beautifully clear.

Another option is the tiny beach underneath the Hotel Bellevue, half of which is public (the other half belongs to the hotel). It's on a gorgeous little cove facing southeast, and hosts Dubrovnik's annual water-polo championships – each little beach and cove around the city has its own team.

For pure hedonistic beach-games and watersports you can't do better than the Copacabana beach on Babin Kuk, though in high season it does get mighty crowded with the package tours from the Babin Kuk hotel complex taking up most of the space. Finally, the Uvala Bay beach, on Lapad, is the locals' beach of choice, and offers lovely swimming out to sea between Babin Kuk and Lapad.

Beaches

Shopping

Dubrovnik's no city for bargain hunters, with prices for most goods being pretty much in line with those across the EU. If you've forgotten to bring something with you, it'll be fairly easy to replace, but you're probably not going to need to bring extra suitcases for all the things you bought here on the cheap.

My faithful 1967 guide to the city advises that 'Peasant and oriental handicrafts are the most popular purchases of visitors to Dalmatia and you will find beautiful leather goods, wood carvings, embroidery, ceramics, silver filigree, brilliantly dyed wool carpets and rugs, and hand-operated coffee grinders made from old artillery shells.' Apart from the first word and the last phrase, it's still pretty accurate nearly 40 years later.

OPENING HOURS AND PDV (VAT)

Opening hours vary but you can expect most shops to be open from 08.00 or 09.00 until 20.00 in the summer. In winter, opening hours tend to be shorter and shops may well close for lunch.

Purchase tax (PDV, or VAT) is set at a flat rate of 22% on all goods except books and essentials. In theory foreigners can get this reimbursed on single-ticket items costing over 500 kuna, but you have to really want the money. Fill in the PDV-P form at the point of sale and get it stamped, so that when you leave Croatia you can have the goods, receipts and forms certified by the Croatian Customs Service – not a process you should undertake if you're in any kind of a hurry. And that's the easy part. You then post back the certified receipts etc to the shop, along with your bank account details. Within a year or so, bingo, the money reappears. It's worth the hassle, of course, on really big-ticket items – but bear in mind when you're bringing goods back home that you may be subject to import duties or asked to prove you've actually paid the VAT.

HANDICRAFTS AND JEWELLERY

When Rebecca West travelled round Dalmatia in 1937, she spent a good part of her trip buying up antique peasant costumes, while noting that fewer and fewer people were wearing them. This trend has continued unabated to the present day, meaning you're unlikely to see traditional dress being worn at all unless you catch a performance of the Linđo ensemble (see page 131). The beautifully embroidered waistcoats and skirts are still being made, but only really to fill a tourist need. Genuinely old costumes are now sufficiently hard to find – and precious – that you'd have to treat anything advertised as such with a dash of scepticism.

If you're into embroidery and lace there's lots for sale, both in souvenir shops and also in the daily market on Gundulićeva poljana (see below). The shop at Dropčeva 6, between Stradun and Prijeko, has a biggish selection, as does the **Dubrovnik House** on Svetog Dominika, the street leading out to the Ploče gate.

As the 1967 guide said, there are lots of places to buy ethnic handicrafts, though they're as likely to come these days from Asia and Africa as from the Balkans.

There's quite a striking variety available at the **Yes Shop**, at Boškovićeva 2, just off Stradun.

You'll also see lots of places selling jewellery, in particular the local silver and gold filigree. Buy this because you like it, not because of the implied value in the precious metal. The **Silver Centar**, at Boškovićeva 6, has a good selection, as does **Djerdj Čivlak**, at Od Puča 18.

If you're looking for a gift, it's well worth visiting **Lush**, at Široka 4, where you can buy their own hand-made soaps, cosmetics and hair-care products.

Also hand-made are **Niko Radić's** sculptures, which come from his studio in the Lazareti. He specialises in quite charming statues of St Blaise in various materials, which – depending on size etc – go for anything from 40 to 2,500 kuna (with a glass of *travarica* thrown in for good measure). He's a very talented sculptor, in the same vein as Ivan Meštrović or Frano Kršnić, and when I was there in 2004 there was an excellent portrait in the studio of the 1920s Croatian firebrand Stjepan Radić – no relation, apparently.

Finally, you should check out the work of **Niko Čučković**, who makes gorgeous designer glassware up in Ploče (he and his Californian-Croatian spouse, Kathy, also have great private rooms for rent – see page 111), under the VitrumDesign brand. The artefacts range from wonderful modern glass plates and dishes to glass-framed mirrors and charming little sailboats made of local pebbles with a pair of tinted-glass sails. Contact Niko at Put Petra Krešimira IV 31; tel: 312 646; mob: 091 769 3993; email: vitrum-design@du.htnet.hr.

BOOKS AND MUSIC

When you run out of holiday reading you shouldn't have too much trouble finding something to replenish your stock here – though expect to pay about 20% over the cover price for books in English. There are some well-produced local books about Dubrovnik which can make good souvenirs or gifts. You sometimes see English books amongst the secondhand collection in the small arcade leading to the cinema next to the Gradska Kavana.

If you get hooked on the local music – and it happens – make sure you buy this before you leave the country. There's a whole Croatian pop- and rock-music scene, as well as the traditional folk music, but even in an online world Croatian music is pretty hard to come by. CDs are about the same price as in most of the EU – perhaps 10% cheaper than in the UK. A good shop to visit is Algoritam (www.algoritam.hr) on Placa 8 which has a wide selection of books and CDs.

MARKETS AND SUPERMARKETS

Dubrovnik has two daily markets, one in the old town and one at Gruž. The old town market takes place on Gundulićeva poljana and includes everything from home-grown fruit, vegetables and flowers, to freshly caught fish, to hand-made lace, to home-distilled *travarica*. The city's main market – aimed very much at locals – is between the port at Gruž and the bus station. You have to get up pretty early to buy the best of the fresh fish here, but fruit, vegetables and flowers go on being wonderfully colourful all morning. There are supermarkets all over town, but the

Mediator chain has three shops just where they're needed for the old town – one outside the Pile gate, one outside the Ploče gate, and one on Gundulićeva poljana. Any of them will make you up a sandwich to order, and they're the obvious place to buy picnic food and anything you want to drink.

For a more upmarket selection of alcoholic beverages try the **Vinoteka**, about halfway along Stradun on the left-hand side coming in from Pile. There's also a reasonable range of drinks available at the duty-free shop at the airport, along with an excellent selection of truffles – but you do need to know (as always with truffles) exactly what you're buying.

FASHION AND ACCESSORIES

You'll see designer labels all over Dubrovnik, both on people and in the shops, though – to judge by the prices, anyway – not everything for sale may be entirely all it's branded to be. With that in mind, you can nonetheless get a fine range of handbags at **Salon Kože 'M'**, on Gundulićeva poljana, and you'll see men's ties for sale all over the place, Croatia being the place where they were invented (see page 29).

There's a trendy shoe shop called **JegerStar** at Od Puča 7, just up and across the street from the Pučić Palace, and there's a branch of **Benetton** in the little arcade by the clocktower, next to Gradska Kavana. There's more Benetton at the **DOC** shopping centre on Kralja Zvonimira in Lapad, which has a range of clothes shops and is the place where you'll find local people doing their own shopping.

Walking Tours

Dubrovnik is the perfect city for walking around – neither too big nor too small – and provides a wealth of hidden historical details in every street and alley. Motor-traffic of all kinds is strictly banned after 10.00, and you can't get lost.

This chapter details two walks – one around the top of the city walls and the other around the old city. Further suggestions for walks can be found at the end of the next chapter.

WALK ONE: AROUND THE CITY WALLS

Dubrovnik's walls are arguably the city's biggest single selling point, and are among the best-preserved and most picturesque in the world. Most importantly, there's a promenade along their entire length, and you should make every effort to circumperambulate at least once, as it really gives you the best possible perspective (physical and historical) of just what Dubrovnik really means.

Altogether there are five gates in the walls, three landward and two on to the harbour (one out to the fish market, the other out by the Rector's Palace to the Ponta quay). The main gates are Pile to the west and Ploče to the east. There's also a new gate called Buža (meaning 'hole'), in the north wall, which was created only a century ago.

The walls surround the entire old town and run for a whisper under 2km. At their highest they're 25m tall, and at their fattest 12m thick. There are five fortresses and around 20 towers. Work started on the walls in the 8th century and continued more or less continuously until the 16th, though much more than you might imagine is also late-20th-century restoration – even before the Serb shells pounded the city in 1991–92. Indeed, when I was here in the 1980s, the promenade around the walls wasn't actually complete. Since the war, a huge amount of restoration has been done throughout the old city, including the complete re-paving of Stradun – not that you'd know – and the replacing of most of the houses' roof-tiles.

There are three places where you can get up on to the walls – on Stradun, right next to the Pile gate; on Svetog Dominika, the road leading up to the Dominican Monastery; and on Kneza Damjana Jude, near the aquarium. The walls are open from 09.00 to 19.00 in summer, with slightly shorter hours in winter, and the entrance fee is 30 kuna. The earlier you get up on to the walls the less crowded you'll find them.

The whole circuit takes a leisurely hour or so if you stop to take pictures (and you will).

To the Minčeta fortress

The route described here starts at the Pile gate and runs clockwise around the town. Climb up the steps to the ticket booth, and you'll see a long flight of steps in front of you heading up to the highest point on the walls, the Minčeta fortress. It's a steep walk up, but well worth the hike as the view from the top is one of the grandest in the city. The fortress was built to an original design by the Italian architect Michelozzo Michelozzi, and was completed in 1465 by the Renaissance genius Juraj Dalmatinac (George the Dalmatian – who was also responsible for the magnificent Renaissance cathedral in Šibenik, among other projects).

Towards the Revelin fortress

The walk along the walls east from the Minčeta fortress, dropping gradually down, offers endless photo opportunities (including the one that's on the cover of this book), and you should take time to dawdle along here. After passing above the Dominican Monastery, the walls loop round to the right, defended by the mass of the Revelin fortress, which was built in the first decades of the 16th century; today it's mainly used for musical performances.

To St John's fortress

The walls now run along the old harbour, skirting the back of the belltower, the Gradska Kavana, the theatre and the **Rector's Palace**, and giving great views over the port. They then take a sharp left out towards St John's (Sveti Ivan's) fortress, which marks the southern defence of Dubrovnik. Built in several stages, from the mid-14th to mid-16th centuries, it today houses the **Aquarium** (see page 160) and the **Maritime Museum** (see page 159).

To the Bokar fortress

You now take a U-turn and start walking west, along the sea walls. Note the occasional figures of St Blaise set into niches on the outside walls, protecting the city. There are marvellous views out to the island of **Lokrum** (see page 175) on the first section, before you turn further west, heading towards the Bokar fortress, which marks the southwestern corner of the city. Inside the walls along this section you get to see something of local life, with washing fluttering on the line, small gardens and terraces, and the leftover ruins of nobles' houses which were destroyed not by the recent war but by the 1979 earthquake.

The Bokar fortress, like the Minčeta, was built to designs by Michelozzo Michelozzi. Originally intended to protect the entrance to Dubrovnik's old harbour, by the time it was completed in 1570 the old town port had already moved around to the other side of the city (where it still is today). From the end of the 18th century the Bokar fortress served as the state prison and asylum.

Across the harbour, on a promontory, is the imposing **Lovrijenac fortress**, also dating from the 15th to 16th centuries. At the entrance there's a famous hexameter, reading '*non bene pro toto libertas venditur auro*'. Translated roughly as 'Liberty cannot be sold for all the gold in the world', it's ironic that it was only the regular payment of gold tributes to the Hungarian kings and the Ottoman sultans which kept Dubrovnik free for so long. Today the fortress is used during the Summer Festival for wonderfully atmospheric productions of *Hamlet* and other Shakespeare classics.

WALK TWO: THE OLD CITY

This walk starts outside the Pile gate and works its way back and forth across the old city, ending at St Blaise's Church. At a leisurely pace – and without stopping for any length of time to admire the attractions or visit museums and churches – it would take about an hour and a half to two hours. If you dip into a handful of the main sights you should count on a good half-day; if you want a detailed visit to everything on the itinerary you'll need a couple of full days at least.

Along Stradun

The busy square outside the Pile gate serves as the start of many an itinerary. At the entrance to the Brsalje terrace, where you'll find both the Nautika restaurant (see page 125) and the Kavana Dubravka (see page 129), there's a distinctive sculpture by Ivan Rendić of a scene from the epic poem *Osman* by Ivan Gundulić, Dubrovnik's favourite poet (see page 152).

The **Pile gate**, dating back to 1471, is approached across a wooden drawbridge which used to be pulled up every night. Set into a niche here is the first of many statues you'll see of St Blaise (Sveti Vlaho), the city's patron saint (see page 3). Indeed, as you enter the gate you'll immediately see another – this time by Ivan Meštrović, Croatia's most famous sculptor. Before World War II there was another relief here as well – you can see where it once was – featuring King Petar Karađorđević and entitled *The Liberator*. That it hasn't survived will come as no great surprise (see page 19).

Stradun

Once inside the gate you come straight on to Dubrovnik's famous main street, **Stradun**, which is paved in marble (be careful when it's wet; it can be lethally slippery). This was originally the marshy channel which separated the Roman settlement of Ragusa on one side from the Slavic settlement of Dubrovnik on the other (see page 5).

On the square inside the Pile gate stands **Onofrio's Great Fountain**, which was completed in 1444 by the Neapolitan architect Onofrio della Cava as part of the city's complex plumbing (see page 13). Unfortunately all the fancy ornamental work from the upper part of the fountain was lost in the Great Earthquake of 1667 (see page 7).

To your left as you come into the city is the tiny **Church of Our Saviour** (Sveti Spas, see page 171), which is used as a perfect venue for candlelit concerts, while next door is the **Franciscan Monastery** (see page 161), home to one of Europe's oldest pharmacies.

Stradun itself (also known as Placa – pronounced *platsa*) continues in a widening straight line all the way to the clocktower at the far end. As you'll notice, the houses along the street are nearly identical, a result of the careful post-earthquake planning at the end of the 17th century. Note the distinctive *'na koljeno'* single-arched frame which combines the entrance door and window to provide a counter over which goods could be served to customers.

Clocktower

In the Luža square, at the far end of Stradun, you'll find **Orlando's Column**, a statue of Roland symbolising the city's desire for freedom (*libertas*) and which has marked the centre of town since its erection in 1418. For centuries Roland's forearm was Ragusa's standard measure of length (the *lakat*, since you ask), a convenient 512mm long – you can see the reference groove at the base of the statue. All state declarations were read from a platform above the column in the days of the republic, and condemned criminals were executed at its base.

On the left-hand side of the square is the **Sponza Palace** (see page 157), which functioned variously as a cistern, the customs house and the state mint. Today it houses the Memorial Room of the Dubrovnik Defenders, the original innards of the city clock, and the State Archives.

Behind Orlando's Column you can't miss the **Clocktower**, originally built in 1444, which features a complex astronomical clock, and a pair of green men (the *zelenci*) who strike the hour. The tower was rebuilt in 1929 (which is presumably when the digital clock was added), so the only thing that's original now is the bell, dating from 1506, which weighs over two tonnes. The original clock mechanism and green men are in the Sponza Palace. Next to the clock tower is **Onofrio's Small Fountain**, dating from 1441.

Orlando's Column

Walk two: the old city

Out to Ploče

From Luža head out past the Sponza Palace and up the winding Svetog Dominika, which leads to the **Dominican Monastery** (see page 162) and the **Ploče gate.** The balustrade of the steps up to the monastery is curiously walled in, up to a height of about two feet – to protect the modesty of travellers and save the monks from impure ankle-related thoughts.

The Ploče gate is a complex structure actually comprising several gates and bridges which were built in the 15th century – though the current design dates from 1628. There's the familiar statue of St Blaise, and a drawbridge leading out into what used to be a market square. As my 1967 guide says: 'Market-goers who spurn modern means of transport still tether their donkeys on the open space where the Moslems from the interior once held their market.'

The main road leads up to the **Lazareti**, Dubrovnik's quarantine houses. Dubrovnik was one of the first ports in Europe to introduce quarantine restrictions, and if you wanted to visit you had to spend 40 days here first before being allowed in. These days the houses and courtyards are used as artists' studios and performance spaces. Further up the hill, on the left-hand side, is Dubrovnik's excellent **Museum of Modern Art** (see page 173).

Along Prijeko

Re-enter the city through the Ploče gate, and turn right up the steps to the Dominican Monastery. At the top of the steps turn left and you'll find yourself at the eastern end of Prijeko, which is best visited early in the day, before the eager restaurateurs can get their teeth into you (see page 118). Take a detour down Žudioska, where you'll find one of Europe's oldest (and smallest) synagogues (see page 172).

Continue down Prijeko for most of its length – or if it's already approaching lunchtime consider avoiding the touts by walking along the old city's uppermost street, Peline, which gives great views down the steep-stepped streets crossing Prijeko – and then turn left down Antuninska, where you'll find the extraordinary **Dubrovnik War Photo** gallery (see page 174).

Coming out on to Stradun, turn right, go back past Onofrio's Great Fountain, and pop into the cloisters of the **Monastery of St Clare** – now rather more prosaically the Jadran restaurant (see page 119).

To Gundulićeva poljana

Come back out of the cloisters and walk around the outside of the monastery along Garište and left on to Za Rokom, where you'll find the little **Church of St Roc**. Round on the right-hand wall of the church is a fine piece of carved graffiti dated 1597 and reading 'PAX VOBIS MEMENTO MORI QUI LUDETIS PILLA' – which translates roughly as 'Peace be with you, but remember that you must die, you who play ball here', clearly the work of an irate adult, keen to warn off noisy football-mad kids.

Continue along Za Rokom until you get to the end of the street, then turn left into Široka. On the right-hand side you'll find the house where **Marin Držić** (see

MARIN DRŽIĆ – DUBROVNIK'S REBELLIOUS PLAYWRIGHT

Born into a large family of merchants in 1508, Marin Držić was originally destined for the Church, and after being ordained at the age of 18 he was sent to Siena to study Church law. He was soon thrown out for his involvement with the theatre, and returned home to Dubrovnik, where he wrote his first plays. These weren't popular with the nobles, who rightly saw the Držić comedies for the political vehicles they were – and presumably weren't wild about being portrayed as inbred fools either.

The latter part of the playwright's life is somewhat of a mystery, though we know that he left Dubrovnik and took up something of a crusade against it. He even wrote a series of letters to the Medicis in Florence, asking them to help him overthrow the republic – though he never received an answer, and died in Venice in poverty in 1567.

Needless to say once Držić was safely out of the way his reputation was quickly rehabilitated, and today his plays – and in particular *Dundo Maroje* – form a central part of the Dubrovnik Summer Festival.

above, and page 160) once lived – although unless you're a serious fan of the playwright's work, you won't get a great deal out of a visit.

Take the next right and walk down Od Puča, where you'll find the **Orthodox Church** on your left, and (two doors down) the **Icon Museum** (see page 170). This part of town is where most of the small remaining Serbian community lives and works. Just down Miha Pracata, on the left-hand side, you'll also find Dubrovnik's **mosque**, which is open from 10.00 to 13.00 daily – though there's really nothing special to see.

Continuing down Od Puča brings you past the Pučić Palace hotel (see page 97) and out on to Gundulićeva poljana – literally Gundulić's little field. In the centre of the square stands a statue of **Ivan Gundulić** himself (see box overleaf), which dates back to 1893. There's a marvellous allegorical vignette at the base of the statue; a bethroned Dubrovnik has both Turkey and Venice at her feet – with Turkey represented as the dragon on the left and Venice as the winged lion on the right. A certain irony, therefore, that the city's most expensive hotel, the Pučić Palace, overlooking the very same square, should today be Turkish-owned.

To the port

Turn right out of Gundulićeva poljana and head up the great flight of steps – said to be modelled on the Spanish Steps in Rome – leading to the **Jesuit Church** (see page 167). Continue out of the far corner of the rather tatty square in front of the church and wind your way all the way along Ispod mira, the alley leading along the inside of the city walls. This is perhaps the quietest and shabbiest part of the town, with lots of buildings still unrestored after being badly damaged in the 1979 earthquake.

Walk two: the old city

IVAN GUNDULIĆ – MASTER OF BAROQUE POETRY

Ivan Gundulić was born in Dubrovnik in 1589, and was famous even in his lifetime as a remarkable poet, churning out vast quantities of – perhaps excessively rhetorical? – baroque verse. Coming from a prominent noble family, it's likely he would have eventually become rector, but he died in 1638, just a few months before the 50th birthday which would have made him eligible.

Gundulić played an important part in standardising the Croatian language, and was enthusiastically taken up by the Croatian Nationalist Movement in the 19th century – indeed it was only then that the great lyrical poem *Osman* was finally finished, with the last two chapters being penned by Ivan Mažuranić, who later went on to become the Ban of Croatia.

As well as being honoured by the statue in Dubrovnik, a fetchingly bewigged Gundulić also appears on the 50-kuna note.

You can now cut across the end of the town, passing the **Aquarium** (see page 160) and the **Maritime Museum** (see page 159) before ducking through on to the quayside. Take a moment here to walk around under St John's fortress and out on to the **Porporela**, where you'll find a compass at the end of the mole, inscribed with the words *Znanje*, *Vjera* and *Srčanost* – Knowledge, Faith and Courage. Back in the days of the republic a chain was stretched nightly from the fortress to the breakwater to protect the harbour.

The heart of the republic

Walk back along the quay to Ponta – where you'll find **Lokanda Peskarija** (see page 120) – and through the city gate to the **cathedral** (see page 164), which is well worth a visit, if only for the treasury. With the cathedral on one side of the square and the **Rector's Palace** (see page 154) on the other, this is really the heart of the republic. Next door is the municipal **theatre**, which was opened in 1869 and features a ceiling by the ubiquitous Vlaho Bukovac (see page 188). It's a charming miniature version of the grand Austro-Hungarian opera houses and theatres, complete with gilded boxes and velvet seating.

Opposite the theatre, and completing the walk in a suitably symbolic fashion, is the **Church of St Blaise** (see page 166).

Museums and Sightseeing

The two best ways of seeing Dubrovnik are from the outside – from the massive town walls, or from the top of Srđ (412m). Time was, you could take a cable-car all the way up – and it's to be hoped that the war damage is repaired soon and it's pressed back into service, as the walk up the barren hillside can be a punishing one (see page 181). For more details on the wonderful 2km promenade around the city walls see page 141.

Once you've seen Dubrovnik from above, choose your time of day for the city itself with care; after 11.00 there's a predictable tendency towards more visitors and less atmosphere – though early evening is a lovely time, regardless of the crowds, with soft light treating old stone kindly.

There's a lot to see in the old city, but don't be too obsessive – not all of the 48 churches within the walls need a visit (or indeed are open), and the museums are mostly fairly low-key. The main sight to see in the end is the city itself – and a trip out to the island of Lokrum (see page 175) can well prove more rewarding than ticking off everything in the following pages…

The attractions in each section are listed, very roughly speaking, in order of merit.

MUSEUMS
The Rector's Palace [1 D3]
Open 09.00–18.00 daily (closes earlier in winter); entry 20 kuna. [1 D3]

Right at the heart of the republic, with the cathedral to one side and St Blaise's Church to the other, is the seat of Ragusa's government, the Rector's Palace (*Knežev Dvor*). It would once have looked more like a castle than a palace, but after the original was accidentally blown up in 1435 (always a mistake keeping your gunpowder next to your government) it was rebuilt in the Venetian-Gothic style by Onofrio della Cava – he of the fountains fame.

It wasn't to last, as the gunpowder went off again in 1463. This time the palace was restored by Michelozzo Michelozzi, who also did lots of work on the city's defensive fortresses, and Juraj Dalmatinac, who added various Renaissance touches.

You enter through a fine loggia topped with superb carved capitals on pillars of Korčula marble; the outer pairs are the original Gothic while the middle three are Renaissance. Most interesting of all is the rightmost capital, thought to portray Aesculapius, the God of Healing, who was born in Epidaurus (now Cavtat).

The main door leads into an atrium which is the (surprisingly small) venue for summer recitals. In here you'll find the only statue ever raised to an individual in Ragusa's long history. On dying in 1607, Miho Pracat (see page 195), a remarkable ship owner and adventurer from Lopud, left 1,000 shares in the Bank of St George in Genoa to the city. The city was suitably grateful – back then those shares were worth around 100 lira apiece, at a time when gold was fetching three and a half lira an ounce. The interest on the capital was used by the city to free slaves, and Pracat got his statue.

The ground floor of the palace was formerly a prison, handy for the courtroom off to the right, with a curious marble barrier and wooden bench being about all you can see today. Upstairs are the state offices and rector's chambers – from the day they were elected, rectors were effectively prisoners here, only allowed to leave with the senate's permission. Fortunately each only served a one-month term.

The main staircase was only used for the rector's inaugural procession on the first of the month, taking him upstairs to his confinement. Nobody ever came down them unless the rector died in office – the hidden staircase behind was the way out. On your way up the main stairs notice the handrails, supported by realistic (if not entirely tasteful) carved hands.

At the top of the stairs, over the door which originally led into the Grand Council chamber, there's an inscription reading *'Obliti Privatorum Publica Curate'* – a quote from Pericles, reminding councillors to forget their private concerns and think of public affairs instead.

The upstairs rooms are a curious collection – mainly because the palace was plundered, first by the French in the early 19th century, and then again by Yugoslavia's King Aleksandar after World War I, for the Royal Palace in Belgrade. As a result they're for the most part furnished with private donations. You'll find an odd mix of Venetian repro, Louis XV copies, painted wood, Neapolitan ebony and marble veneer, along with an unusual collection of canvasses featuring local bigwigs. Note also the keys to the city – the gates were locked every night and the keys were kept in the rector's office – and the candlelit clock.

The Sponza Palace [1 D2/D3]

The Sponza Palace, facing St Blaise's Church, is one of the most charming buildings in Dubrovnik, boldly mixing pure Venetian Gothic and late Renaissance into a harmonious whole. It was built in 1522 to plans by the local architect Pasko Miličević, and features work by the Andrijić brothers, the master sculptors who were also responsible for much of Korčula Cathedral – as well as the Church of Our Saviour at the other end of Stradun. The Sponza was one of the few buildings to survive the Great Earthquake of 1667.

The entrance is through a wide-arched Renaissance portico, above which there's a lovely Venetian-Gothic first storey, topped with a row of four late-Renaissance windows and a statue of St Blaise in a niche. Inside there's a courtyard with a double cloister.

The name Sponza comes from the Latin word *spongia*, meaning sponge, as there was originally a cistern on this site. The Sponza's main purpose, however, was to serve as the republic's customs house (which is why it's also sometimes referred to as the Divona or Dogana). On the ground floor here goods were measured for duty, under the inscription *'Fallere Nostra Vetant et Falli Pondera Meque Pondero cum Merces Ponderat ipse Deus'* – which translates roughly as 'the scales we use to weigh your goods are the same scales used by God to weigh us'.

The ground-floor rooms originally served as warehouse space, while those on the first floor were used for literary and scientific meetings. Up on the second floor

Museums

was the state mint, which issued Dubrovnik's currency (*perperae*, *grossi* and *ducats*) from 1337 until 1803.

After World War II, the Sponza housed the Museum of the Socialist Revolution, though of course that's disappeared following the more recent war. Instead you'll find the original 16th-century mechanism for the city clock here, along with the two green men, Maro and Baro, who struck the bell until 1928. The space is used for concerts during the Summer Festival.

The Sponza also houses two museums, the Memorial Room of the Dubrovnik Defenders and the State Archives.

Memorial Room of the Dubrovnik Defenders

On the ground floor of the Sponza you'll find a commemoration of the tragic events here from October 1 1991 to October 26 1992, when more than 200 defenders and 100 civilians were killed. It's a terribly sobering place, with the remnants of the flag from the Imperial Fort on Srđ and the pictures and dates of all the young lives which were snuffed out during the siege. The room is open from 08.00 to 14.00 daily.

State Archives

Dubrovnik's State Archives are among the most complete in the world, and chronicle pretty much everything that happened during the 1,000-year history of the republic. Altogether there are some 8,000m of shelved documents, ranging from 13th-century city statutes to Marshal Marmont's orders dissolving the republic in 1808. The archives are open to researchers from 07.00 to 14.00 daily – you should call ahead or email in advance if you want to visit (tel: 321 032; email: arhiv-dubrovnik@dad.hr).

Maritime Museum [1 E3/E4]

Open Tue–Sun 09.00–19.00 (shorter hours in winter); entry 15 kuna

Dubrovnik's Maritime Museum is housed out at the end of Kneza Damjana Jude in St John's fortress, upstairs from the aquarium. Spread out over two floors, the museum covers the entire history of seafaring in the area, from the Golden Age of the Republic through to the arrival of steam-powered ships. It's well worth a visit if you're into ships and sailing, with lots of maps, evocative old photos and models of various types of ship, along with bits of rigging and ships' supplies and cargoes.

Rupe Ethnographic Museum [1 A3]

Open 09.00–18.00 daily; entry 10 kuna

As part of its defensive strategy – one which was virtually never needed, as it happened – Dubrovnik had numerous granaries around town, capable of holding enough food to withstand a serious siege. The last-remaining one of these is now the Rupe museum (*rupe* means 'holes'), and you can see some of the vast chambers which were dug into the rock to store grain back in the 16th century, keeping the food dry and cool – the temperature is steady year-round at 18°C.

Museums

Upstairs there's a moderately interesting ethnographic museum, giving you a taste of peasant life in the past – which here, as everywhere else, looks like it was pretty rough.

Home of Marin Držić [1 B3]

Open Mon–Sat 09.00–14.00; entry 10 kuna

Marin Držić (see box on page 150) was one of Croatia's most famous playwrights, and you can visit his house here in Dubrovnik. Unfortunately there's not all that much to see, and unless you're a big fan of his work, you won't get a great deal out of the visit – which depends mainly on an audio-visual presentation of 16th-century life in the republic.

Aquarium [1 E3/E4]

Open 10.00–20.00 daily (10.00–13.00 in winter); entry 20 kuna

Housed downstairs from the Maritime Museum, in St John's fortress, there's no reason, in such an atmospheric setting, why Dubrovnik's sea-water aquarium shouldn't be fabulous – indeed my handy 1967 guide to the city describes it as 'magnificent'.

If it ever was the case, it's magnificent no more – in fact it's simply dismal. Mostly it amounts to large Mediterranean fish (groupers, eels and the like) swimming listlessly round in tanks that don't seem big enough. The whole bleak experience is epitomised by the solitary giant turtle which paddles its way to and fro miserably in a pond-sized pool, while school groups chuck small change at the benighted beast.

MONASTERIES AND CHURCHES
The Franciscan Monastery [1 A2/B2]
Open 09.00–17.00; entry 10 kuna

Early in the 14th century the Franciscans were granted a plot of land just inside the city walls (they had previously been outside the Pile gate, where the Hilton Imperial is now) and they wasted no time in building their monastery. The Franciscan Monastery is entered from Stradun itself, where you'll find the south door crowned by a wonderful Pietà – evocatively described by Rebecca West in 1937 as 'definite and sensible. The Madonna looks as if, had it been in her hands, she would have stopped the whole affair.'

The Pietà survived the Great Earthquake, but the church itself was entirely gutted by fire and countless treasures were lost forever. What you see today dates from the 18th century onwards, which explains the baroque nature of it all – though it's hard not to have a soft spot for St Francis, praying while foxes and rabbits peacefully co-exist in the background. The church is famous locally as the final resting place of Ivan Gundulić (see page 152), though he's actually interred in a part of the church which is closed to the public – you can still pay your respects at a plaque on the north wall, however. As you'd expect, the church makes an excellent venue for concerts during the Summer Festival.

The rest of the monastery is accessed down a narrow passage next to the Church of Our Saviour (see page 171). At the entrance you'll find the famous pharmacy, self-billed as the oldest in the world. Whether it is or not, it probably was one of the earliest to be open to the public, and it's still operating today, though from a 1901 refurbishment (open Mon–Sat 08.00–14.00). The original pharmacy was established in 1317, and in the museum off the cloisters you can see an interesting collection of jars and poisons from the 15th century on, along with ancient pharmacopoeias. The museum also contains various religious artefacts, as well as a testy portrait of Ruđer Bošković, Dubrovnik's mathematical genius (see page 16), painted in 1760 in London. Most interesting of all is a canvas showing the old town before the earthquake – note how much greater Onofrio's Great Fountain was before 1667.

The cloisters themselves are truly exceptional, consisting of rows of double octagonal columns with individualised capitals. They are the work of Mihoje Brakov, a sculptor from Bar (in what's now Montenegro), who died here of the plague in 1348. One of the capitals near the entrance, depicting a medieval man with terrible toothache, is said to be a self-portrait of the sculptor himself. Inside the courtyard are palm trees and well-trimmed box hedges, and it's a great place to get away from the heat in high summer.

The Dominican Monastery [1 D2]
Open 09.00–17.00 daily; entry 15 kuna

The Dominican Monastery comprises a big church, a set of lovely cloisters and an excellent museum. The monastery was used by the occupying French troops from 1808 – you can see from the outside where windows were sealed up to make a Napoleonic prison, and the church itself was used as stables. In the cloisters you can still see the horse troughs which were hacked into the retaining walls by the cavalrymen.

The original church here was completed in 1315, but had to be rebuilt after the Great Earthquake of 1667. It was paved with the coats of arms of all the noble families, but unfortunately was then repaved in 1910 with plain marble. Today it's a vast, boxy place, and most of the best artworks have been moved to the museum – though not the greatest treasure of all, a terrific 5m x 4m crucifixion by Paolo Veneziano, which was installed here in 1358. There's also an interesting painting of St Dominic by local boy Vlaho Bukovac, though it's not, frankly, the artist's best work – you can see some of this at the Museum of Modern Art (see page 173) in Dubrovnik, and even more in the painter's home town, Cavtat (see page 184). During the Summer Festival, the church plays host to numerous concerts.

The cloisters are a late-Gothic masterpiece, built to a design by the Florentine architect Maso di Bartolomeo, but with extra flourishes added by local stonemasons. In the courtyard oranges and lemons grow, and – like the Franciscan cloisters – it's a wonderfully cool, shady place on a hot day.

The monastery itself houses an interesting museum and an extraordinary library; with over 16,000 works and 240 incunabula, it was one of the greatest European libraries of the Renaissance. In the museum you'll find a rare 11th-century Bible, along with a much-reproduced triptych featuring St Blaise with a model of pre-earthquake Ragusa in his right hand – still recognisable as Dubrovnik today, though both the Franciscan and Dominican monasteries sported bigger spires back then. Also of note is a marvellous altarpiece by Titian featuring Mary Magdalene with St Blaise and the Archangel Raphael – the chap on his knees is the member of the Pučić family who commissioned the work.

Up a couple of stairs there's a room full of votive gold – a fraction of what was here originally, as most of it was sold off after World War II to support the faculty of theology, unfunded in communist times. There's an interesting Flemish diptych here – with Jesus on the left while on the right there's a reversible panel, with love on one side and death on the other.

The Cathedral [1 D4]

Usually open 08.00–20.00; entrance to the treasury 5 kuna

Dubrovnik's Romanesque cathedral – said to have been bankrolled by a shipwrecked Richard the Lionheart (see box, page 168) – was demolished by the Great Earthquake in 1667, so what you get today is the baroque replacement, which was completed in 1713 to plans by the Italian architect Andrea Buffalini. The statues of the saints along the eaves are rather fine, though notice that St Mark has been relegated to an inferior position – perhaps a none-too-subtle snub to Venice.

Surprisingly, for baroque, the cathedral is a rather spartan affair inside, with a chunky modern altar and acres of whitewash – and it's curious in having a west-facing altar. The compelling attraction is the treasury, though if you're here it's nonetheless worth having a look at the impressive (school of) Titian altarpiece.

The cathedral treasury

'The beauty and richness of this holy place is a wonder to all who visit it,' said French Ambassador Jean de Gontaut Biron, when he came through in 1604 – and it's hard to disagree, even if to modern sensibilities the grisliness of the treasury tends to overshadow its 'beauty and richness'.

Altogether, there are well over 100 priceless relics here, many of which are carried around the town in a grand procession on February 3, St Blaise's feast day. The most important of these is the head of St Blaise himself, which was bought from Byzantium (along with the saint's arms and a leg) in 1026. The head is housed in a fine casing decorated with 24 Byzantine enamel plaques from the 12th century, featuring austere, intense portraits of the saints.

The treasury also includes one of John the Baptist's hands, a bit of the True Cross incorporated into a crucifix, one of Christ's nappies in a silver box, and a dark wooden lectern which once belonged to England's Henry VIII – after the Reformation, treasures from the dissolved monasteries went up for sale, and a small selection ended up in the hands of enterprising sailors from Lopud (see page 192).

Over on the right-hand side is an extraordinary painting by Raphael, the *Madonna della Seggiola* (Sedia), which is almost identical to the 1514 version in the Palazzo Pitti in Florence. Why there's a copy here – painted on what looks like the bottom of a barrel – is a mystery, but the painting itself is a pure wonder.

Last but not least is an extraordinary pitcher and ewer from the 15th century, prominently on display, which is an allegory of Dubrovnik's flora and fauna.

Featuring snakes and tortoises, eels and lizards, and some pre-Dali lobsters, along with alarming amounts of vegetation, it looks like it would be the very devil to clean. It is thought to have been made as a gift for the Hungarian king of the day, Matthias Corvinus the Just, but ended up here as the king died before he could receive the tribute.

It's always aroused a certain amount of passion. In 1929, Count Voynovitch, author of a handy little guide to the city, said: 'The basin is delightfully finished.' Just eight years later, however, Rebecca West was writing: 'Nothing could be more offensive to the eye, to the touch, or to common sense ... it has the infinite elaborateness of eczema, and to add to the last touch of unpleasantness these animals are loosely fixed so that they may wobble and give an illusion of movement. Though Dubrovnik is beautiful, and this object was indescribably ugly, my dislike of the second explained to me why I felt doubtful in my appreciation of the first. The town regarded this horror as a masterpiece.'

And it's true; it does.

The Church of St Blaise (Sveti Vlaho) [1 C3/D3]
Usually open 08.00–20.00

The original church on this site was built in the 14th century, and although it (mostly) survived the Great Earthquake in 1667, it was subsequently consumed by fire. Miraculously, the 15th-century gold and silver statue of St Blaise escaped unharmed.

The new baroque church was completed in 1717 to plans by the Venetian architect Marino Grapelli, who based the interior design on the Church of San Maurizio in his home town. It's even more unusual than the cathedral in its orientation, in having a south-facing altar.

The church is an elegant tribute to the city's patron saint, with a classic baroque façade. Inside it's not as austere as the cathedral but not too over the top either. The main attraction is the altar, where you can admire the famous statue of St Blaise holding the city – which shows you what it looked like in about 1485.

Also worth your attention is the painting across the organ loft representing the Martyrdom of St Blaise, which was painted by local boy Petar Matejević in the early 18th century. Spare a moment too for the stained-glass windows, which depict Saints Peter and Paul and Saints Cyril and Methodius, the creators of the Glagolitic alphabet (a later variant of which, Cyrillic, is named after St Cyril). These are the work of Ivo Dulčić, one of Dubrovnik's most famous modern artists, who died in 1975.

The Jesuit Church [1 C4]

Open 08.00–18.00 daily (often closed at lunchtime)

Physically dominating the old town is the Jesuit church (properly the Church of St Ignatius of Loyola, or Ignacija Lojolskog), a massive structure clearly intended to make a point. It was built to plans by the Jesuit artist Andrea Pozzo, who had already done great works in Rome and would go on to design the cathedral in Ljubljana.

Monasteries and churches

RICHARD THE LIONHEART AND DUBROVNIK

Ask anyone about Dubrovnik's cathedral and it won't be long before Richard the Lionheart's name comes up. According to local legend, the English king ran into a terrible storm near here on his return home from the crusades at the end of 1192, and vowed that if he survived he would build a church on the spot. Miraculously, he was saved, and washed up on Lokrum.

On hearing the news of the arrival of such an important – and apparently loaded – visitor, Dubrovnik sent over a welcoming party, who persuaded King Richard that his money would be better spent on building a cathedral in Dubrovnik. In exchange, the Ragusan nobles would build a votive church on Lokrum at their own expense.

Richard agreed, and handed over 100,000 ducats, before continuing on his journey to Italy and – eventually – England. In all probability, however, the Lokrum part of this charming tale is a Benedictine fabrication.

First of all, the amount of money is far too large. Although work did start on the cathedral in 1199, it wasn't finished until the 14th century, mainly because of a shortage of funds – whereas 100,000 ducats would have been more than enough money for even the most opulent of churches.

What's more, Dubrovnik legend has it that Richard went on to Ancona, but we know he actually came ashore (after another great storm) in Aquileia, between Trieste and Venice. He was then captured in Vienna (in December 1192) and imprisoned in Durenstein castle on the Danube – where he was discovered (according to romantic myth) by his faithful minstrel Blondel. He didn't get back to England until 1194.

The Benedictine monks on Lokrum had good cause for inventing – or at the very least embellishing – such a story. Because of it, they enjoyed various privileges in Dubrovnik's cathedral, including the abbot of Lokrum being allowed to hold the Candlemas pontifical mass, which is celebrated on February 2, the day before St Blaise's feast day. This mass apparently enraged successive bishops of Dubrovnik, who demanded the privilege be rescinded. In the end, in the 1590s, the Dubrovnik government had to resort to writing letters to the pope, who finally decided in favour of Lokrum's Benedictines – thereby legitimising the Lionheart story.

Nonetheless, it's quite likely that Richard the Lionheart did in fact come here, as his route home would have taken him along the Dalmatian coast, and he would probably have dropped in to pay his respects. Being a crusader and a king, it's even possible he made a gift towards the construction of the new cathedral.

Monasteries and churches

Completed in 1725, the church features a dramatic double-storeyed set of Corinthian columns lifting the façade skywards, and the church behind it is enormous, covering a surface of over 600m². A bell dating back to 1355 hangs in the belfry.

Inside it feels very big and gloomy, as you'd expect, with the interior modelled on the Gesù Church in Rome and featuring lots of fabulous *trompe l'oeil*, Pozzi's speciality – he was the author of a seminal work on perspective, *Prospettiva de' pittori et architect*, which revolutionised painting in the 18th century. The main attraction is the inside of the apse, which features spectacular scenes from the life of Ignatius, the founder of the Jesuit order, by the Sicilian painter Gaetano Garcia.

Altogether less spiritually uplifting – though popular enough with local devotees, it seems – is the 'Grotto of Lourdes', which was added in 1885.

Both Ruđer Bošković (see page 16) and Ivan Gundulić (see page 152) were educated at the Jesuit College next door.

The Orthodox Church and Icon Museum [I B3]
Open 09.00–16.00 daily

One of Dubrovnik's most recent churches is the Serbian Orthodox Church of the Holy Annunciation on Od Puča, which was only completed in 1877. A plain exterior shelters a rather spare interior, with a traditional iconostasis (with icons from the 15th to 19th centuries) separating the clergy from the congregation.

The church was one of the last buildings in the old town – perhaps unsurprisingly – on which restoration work got under way after the end of the siege in 1992, but happily is now receiving both attention and funds; hopefully it will be fully restored in the near future.

The Icon Museum
Open Mon–Sat 09.00–13.00; entry 10 kuna
Two doors down, at Od Puča 8, is Dubrovnik's small Icon Museum. The rarely visited museum is upstairs, on the second floor (past a sign in Cyrillic saying СЯПСКА – Srpska, or Serbian). It's a pity as the two-room collection brings together a wide range of icons from the 18th and 19th centuries, as well as some earlier ones from the 15th and 16th centuries. They come from all across the Balkans and Russia and the differences between the various schools are fascinating – the Russian icons featuring long noses; the ones from the Bay of Kotor having deep, dark shadows. In the second room there are also half a dozen dark, dark portraits of local 19th-century Serb notables by Vlaho Bukovac (see page 188), quite unlike anything else you'll see by the famous local painter.

The Church of Our Saviour (Sveti Spas) [1 A2]
Open 09.00–16.00 daily
Set right inside the Pile gate is the little Church of Our Saviour. It was completed in 1528 as a thank you from the survivors of the 1520 earthquake, and itself

survived the far more dramatic quake of 1667 – a tribute to the building skills of the Andrijić brothers, from Korčula, who also worked on the Sponza Palace. The simple Renaissance trefoil façade and rose window are quietly pleasing, and hide a Gothic interior which is mainly used these days as a venue for candlelit concerts.

The Synagogue [1 C2]

Open Mon–Fri 10.00–13.00; entry 10 kuna

Europe's second-oldest synagogue (after Prague) is upstairs in a small house on Žudioska, between Stradun and Prijeko. In spite of restrictions placed on Jews here during World War II, it was the only European synagogue to function all the way through the war.

The Jewish community in Dubrovnik was mentioned for the first time in 1352, and the first Catalan Jew arrived in 1421. After the expulsion of the Jews from Spain in 1492, numbers increased, and around 500 years ago the house here was given to the Jewish community for use as a synagogue – though from 1540 Jews had to wear badges, and from 1546 a ghetto was imposed on them.

The synagogue – with original 17th-century furnishings – is on the second floor, while below it, on the first floor, there's a fascinating two-room museum, where you can see richly decorated Torah Scrolls and binders, and ancient Ark Curtains, as well as a copy of the letter signed by Marshal Marmont granting the Jewish community full emancipation from 1808. There's also a chilling selection of documents from

1941, issued by the fascist NDH (see page 20), restricting the movement of Jews and ordering them to wear yellow ribbons and badges.

GALLERIES
The Museum of Modern Art [2 J3/J4]
Open Tue–Sun 10.00–19.00; entry 20 kuna

Dubrovnik's modern art museum is in Ploče, on the road running up to the Excelsior and Argentina hotels, at Frana Supila 23. Even if there were no art to see, the building itself is magnificent and well worth a visit. Built in 1939 as the summer villa for a wealthy ship owner, Božo Banac, it was erected in a Renaissance style reminiscent of the Rector's Palace and you wouldn't know it wasn't ancient. Since 1950 it has housed the Museum of Modern Art's ever-expanding (and excellent) collection.

The permanent collection includes paintings and sculpture from Croatia's greatest artists as well as focusing on the burgeoning local scene. The collection is rotated and there are usually temporary exhibitions, so what's on show at any one time varies. Look out for sculpture from two of Croatia's most representative and best-known sculptors, Ivan Meštrović and Frano Kršnić, as well as landscapes by Mato Celestin Medović and interiors and still lifes from Emanuel Vidović. The show is stolen, naturally, by Vlaho Bukovac (see page 188), and the gallery holds some of his very best work, including a number of gorgeous, complex portraits – though they're not always all on show.

There are also two publications well worth trying to get hold of. The first, simply titled *Pavo Urban – The Last Shots*, is an emotionally charged book reproducing the pictures taken on the morning of December 6 1991 on a deserted Stradun and Luža square before the photographer, Pavo Urban, was hit and killed by a piece of shrapnel, aged only 23. The second is a moving series of photographic essays by the director of the museum, Antun Maračić, entitled *Emptied Frames, Vanished Contents, 1991–1994*, which chillingly draws attention to the emptiness and abandonment war leaves behind.

War Photo Limited [1 B2]

Open May–Oct 09.00–21.00 daily; in winter (closed Jan–Feb) Mon–Fri 09.00–16.00, Sat 09.00–14.00; entry 25 kuna

Tucked away at Antuninska 6, between Stradun and Prijeko, is one of Dubrovnik's newest and most moving galleries, and I can't recommend a visit too highly. Specialising in first-rate temporary exhibitions by the world's greatest modern-war photographers, the gallery aims, as the New Zealand-born director, Wade Goddard, says: 'to strip away the Hollywood image of war, to replace the glamour, the heroic bravura, the "only the bad guys suffer" image of war, with the raw and undeniable evidence that war inflicts injustices on all who experience it'.

It would require a heart of stone to come away unmoved by the extraordinary (and often painful) images. When I visited in the summer of 2004, Ron Haviv's breathtaking *Blood and Honey* collection was on show – 'bal' being Turkish for 'honey' and *'kan'* being Turkish for 'blood'. Haviv won the 'World Press Photo' award for his iconic pictures of the fall of Vukovar in 1991, and is one of the co-founders of agency vii (see www.viiphoto.com).

Check out www.warphotoltd.com for details of current and upcoming exhibitions.

THE GREAT OUTDOORS

If you want to get away from the city, there are several nearby attractions which will take your mind off the bustle. Easily the best of these is the lovely island of Lokrum, just offshore, and you should make every effort – even on a whistle-stop visit to Dubrovnik – to get out there. Alternatives include the hike up to the top of Srđ, or the promenade around the Babin Kuk peninsula. There's also a lovely walk to be had by heading out through Ploče past the hotels, and then branching right on to Vlaha Bukovaca, past the Villa Dubrovnik hotel and along to the former Monastery of St James, with great views across to Lokrum and back to the old town.

Lokrum

Said to have been visited unwillingly by Richard the Lionheart in 1192 (see the box on page 168) the sub-tropical island of Lokrum is just a 15-minute boat ride away from the old town quay.

The island remains undeveloped, and makes for a wonderful break from the

THE BENEDICTINES' CURSE OF LOKRUM

The monastery on Lokrum was founded in the 11th century, and Benedictine monks lived there peacefully enough (notwithstanding the Lionheart business – see page 168) for the next 800 years. In 1808, however, the republic was dissolved and the French governor ordered the closure of the monastery.

The monks, none too happy about the turn of events, are said to have spent their last night on Lokrum tramping round the shoreline solemnly with upturned candles, chanting a curse that would damn anyone who tried to own the island after their departure.

As legend has it, the curse was quick to take effect, with the first victims being the three hapless nobles who had brought the bad tidings to the Benedictines from the French: one drowned, another was killed by a servant and the third was defenestrated.

In 1859, Lokrum was bought by Maximilian, the brother of the Austro-Hungarian Emperor Franz Josef. He planted tropical gardens, constructed pathways across the island, imported large numbers of exotic birds (hence the peacocks), and is said to have regularly slept in one of the monks' cells. It was all no doubt very peaceful, but in 1864 Maximilian was sent off by his brother to be the Emperor of Mexico. Three years later he was executed there by rebel generals.

According to the legend, the island was then offered for sale to Dubrovnik, but the city wouldn't touch it. The next owner was a wealthy businessman, who rapidly found himself ruined financially. Lokrum passed to one of Franz Josef's most trusted lawyers, who was then swiftly unmasked as a charlatan, and discredited – although he managed to hang on to Lokrum. It passed on to his nephew, who promptly drowned on his way out to inspect the newly inherited property.

Lokrum returned to the royal family in 1880, being taken over by the emperor's only son, Crown Prince Rudolf. Rudolf came to Lokrum on honeymoon with his young wife Stephanie, but later fell fatally in love with Marie Vetsera, with the couple committing a dramatic double suicide in Mayerling on January 30 1889.

Rudolf's mother, Elisabeth (Sisi), in an attempt to lift the curse, is then said to have offered Lokrum back to the Benedictines, but true to their word they wouldn't return. After a botched deal to give the island to the Dominicans, Lokrum passed back to Emperor Franz Josef, and on September 10 1898, in Geneva, his beloved Sisi was stabbed to death by an Italian anarchist.

Her nephew, Archduke Franz Ferdinand, had intended to spend the summer of 1914 on Lokrum with his wife Sophie Chotek – but the pair were assassinated instead in June in Sarajevo, sparking off World War I.

The great outdoors

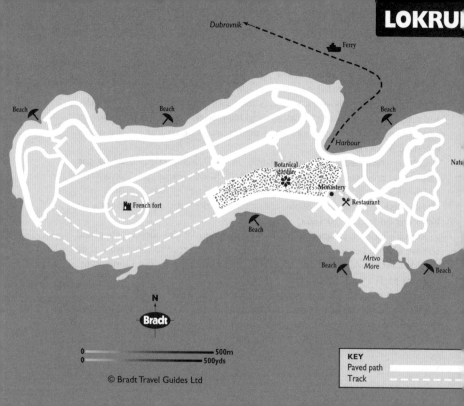

crowds onshore. Even when the boats are arriving full, every half-hour, the 2km-long island can easily absorb all comers, leaving an impression – away from a small central part – of calm and tranquillity, punctuated only by the cries of birds and the fluttering of butterflies.

A network of footpaths criss-crosses the island and provides access to the sea and into the dense woods. There are several rock beaches, and these are cleaner, fresher and less crowded than Dubrovnik's, as well as a warm salt-water lake (*Mrtvo More*, the Dead Sea), on the other side of the island from where the boat arrives. This has a 10m cliff which encourages the local lads to dive off it, apparently without harm. There's a naturist beach on Lokrum, too, on the southeastern end of the island, away from prying eyes.

Lokrum's main attraction lies in its enormous variety of vegetation, which is all the more astonishing when you realise there's no fresh water supply – hence the absolute ban on making fires of any kind and even on smoking. When you're wandering the paths look out for numerous species of birds (including peacocks) and butterflies. On a visit here in June I saw white admirals, several sorts of fritillary, and some skittish large yellows.

In the middle of the island, there's an old botanical garden, most of which seems like a series of wonderfully unmaintained secret gardens. Amongst slightly dilapidated walls you'll find palms with soft furry trunks, trellises of twisted vines and crippled trees supported on crutches, while broken cloches sprout thyme and basil and lettuce run to seed.

The great outdoors

In the heavy silence and deep shade there's an agreeable air of mystery – which is shattered fairly unceremoniously when you round a corner and discover the restaurant and bar, and a small natural history museum, all within the structure of what was once a large Benedictine monastery. You don't need to worry about the Benedictines' curse (see box, page 176) these days, unless of course you're thinking about buying the island.

On the summit of the island – a steepish 20-minute hike – there's a ruined fort. Built by the French in 1808, it gives great views out over Dubrovnik, and the nearby coast and the islands. Be careful here though – it's in a parlous state, and the steps leading inside and up to the lookout are on the point of collapse.

It was from the northern tip of Lokrum that I finally realised what it was I'd found vaguely make-believe about Dubrovnik all along: it's a film set. So many movies have plundered that fortified look – the big walls, the red-roofed houses nestled between them dominated by a smattering of palaces and churches – that it doesn't seem real. It looks like it's meant to be looked at, but could never really have been lived in.

To get to Lokrum, take the half-hourly boat (every day in season, otherwise only on weekends) from the old harbour, and make sure you know what time the last one is coming back. Tickets cost around 30 kuna return. If you're here on a weekday out of season just ask around at the harbour and you'll soon find someone willing to take you across. Expect to pay up to 100 kuna a head, and make sure the skipper knows what time you want to be picked up.

Mount Srđ

Looming large above Dubrovnik, and visible from all over the city, is the mountain of Srđ. Up until 1991 there was a cable-car which whisked visitors up to the top for the incredible view over the city and the islands, but it became one of the first victims of the war.

The cable-car hasn't been put back into service since then – apparently because of a long-running dispute, with the top and bottom stations owned by different companies. It's a great pity, as the only way up now is on foot – unless you happen to have access to a vehicle, in which case you can take the road up to the village of Bosanka, before turning left on to the road to the summit.

If you do decide to walk up, bear in mind that the path is long, steep, and entirely without shade for the last two-thirds. At first it's through pine trees, with butterflies and cicadas – magic and very cool. There's no water to be had, either on the way up or at the top, so take plenty with you. And although the path is perfectly safe, and the hillside is said to be clear of unexploded ordnance, you should stick to the main track just in case.

The path climbs up from the main road running above Dubrovnik – referred to variously as Državna Cesta or Jadranska Cesta (and formerly Put Jugoslavenske Narodne Armije). Starting at the Pile gate, turn right just after the bus stop and work your way up Zrinsko-Frankopanska. Cross over Zagrebačka and then Gornji Kono, then take the next right and follow this slip road under Jadranska Cesta. After this the footpath starts off to your left. From the Pile gate it will take you

The great outdoors

anything between one hour and two, to the top of Mount Srđ, depending on how fit you are.

At the top you'll find the Imperial Fort, which was built by the French in 1810. In the 1970s it became a popular discothèque (rumours that this author was once seen strutting his stuff there many years ago are clearly unfounded). Today, the fort is still badly damaged and can't officially be visited, so the only reason to climb up this far is for the magnificent views – and of course the exercise. What you won't miss is the huge cross at the top, which now dominates the Old Town, especially when it's illuminated at night. As you climb up in the heat, spare a thought for the mothers of those killed in the war who follow the route as a pilgrimage for their sons, walking barefoot to the top and stopping to pray at each of the 13 crosses placed at corners along the way.

Cross above Dubrovnik, Mt Srđ

Lapad and Babin Kuk

For something a little less demanding than the hike up Mount Srđ, there are lovely paths reaching up into the woods of the Lapad peninsula. The easiest place to start is at the Dubrovnik Palace hotel (see page 101), though you can also work your way up from the streets leading off to the left from Ispod Petke to Ivanska. There are two summits, Mala Petka to the west, at 145m, and Velika Petka to the east, at 192m.

There's also an excellent walk which takes you right the way around the Babin Kuk peninsula. This takes about two hours – though it can be a bit fiddly in the height of the season, when the Babin Kuk hotel-complex beaches get crowded.

The path starts at the Casa Bar and Ristorante (see page 129), on Uvala Bay, and winds its way west, past the Levanat restaurant (see page 124). The track ends at the gate (open 08.00–20.00) on to the Dubrovnik President hotel's beach, after which you need to head up a flight of narrow steps to pick up the path again opposite the island of Daksa. Following this brings you to the Copacabana beach and eventually brings you out at the Dubrovnik yacht club. After this you follow the road past the Hotel Lapad, eventually coming out by the bus station.

Beyond the City

Beyond Dubrovnik itself, southern Dalmatia is unusually rich in other sights, from the charming town of Cavtat to the quiet Elaphite islands (Koločep, Lopud and Šipan) and the near-perfection of Mljet, with its national park.

SOUTH OF DUBROVNIK

From Dubrovnik it's 40km south to the Montenegrin border. On the way there's a string of resorts (Kupari, Srebreno, Mlini, Soline and Plat) collectively known as the Župa Dubrovačka, which lead to the town of Cavtat (pronounced *tsavtat*), after which there's just Čilipi airport and a handful of fishing villages before the border.

Cavtat

Situated 16km south, the small, pleasant seaside town of Cavtat makes an excellent and easy excursion from Dubrovnik. There are regular buses and ferries between the two and accommodation is both cheaper and easier to find here. If you're visiting the area by car, Cavtat makes an ideal base, with nothing like the parking hassles you'll find in Dubrovnik itself. The #10 Libertas bus runs about once an hour from 06.00 to midnight, and costs 12 kuna each way (pay on the bus) while the standard ferry runs until 18.00 and costs around 60 kuna return. If their hours don't suit, other ferry companies run to a different timetable, including one that runs a last return trip at 23.45. Rates are the same for all operators.

SOUTHERN DALMATIA

Medugorje

Metković

Ploče

Ferry

Neretva Delta

BOSNIA & HERZEGOVINA

N

Bradt

0 — 16km
0 — 10miles

© Bradt Travel Guides Ltd

MONTENEGRO

Pelješac

Neum
(Bosnia)

Ston

Fast catamaran

mmer
nly

Šipan

Ferry

Slano

Sobra

Šipanska Luka

če

Mljet

Korita

Suđurađ

Trsteno

Trebinje

Lopud

New Bridge

Lopud

Koločep

DUBROVNIK

Lokrum

Adriatic Sea

Cavtat

Čilipi

Ferry

Italian waters

Risan

Perast

Hercog Novi

Cetinje

Bari

Bay of Kotor

▲ *Mt Lovćen*
1749m

Kotor

Cavtat was originally the Greek and then Roman colony of Epidaurus, though there's nothing left at all from that era barring a few classical fragments built into houses – fishermen, in Rebecca West's nicely turned phrase, having 'taken what they would of sculptures and bas-reliefs to build up their cottage walls, where they can be seen today, flowers in the buttonhole of poverty'.

Cavtat (the name seems likely to be derived from the Latin word *civitas*) occupies a peninsula between two bays, and has a charming palm-studded front lined with cafés and restaurants. There's not a whole lot to do, though the **Franciscan Monastery**, at the end of the quay, hides a pair of lovely Renaissance paintings, and the **Rector's Palace**, at the other end of the waterfront, houses the town museum (open Mon–Fri 09.00–13.00; entry 10 kuna) – notable in particular for a selection of excellent works by the local painter **Vlaho Bukovac** (see page 188).

Many more Bukovac paintings can be found at the artist's house, which is now the **Galerija Bukovac**, though if this is the main reason for your visit check ahead, as it was still closed for restoration during 2004. When it reopens, over 80 of the artist's oils, spanning his entire career, will be on show here.

Right at the end of the peninsula, in a gorgeous hilltop location overlooking the sea and surrounded by cypresses, is the town cemetery. Here you'll find one of Cavtat's most important treasures, the **Račić Mausoleum** – though it too was closed for restoration in the summer of 2004. Its commissioning by a daughter of the ship-owning Račić family seems to have been their downfall. No sooner was the building underway than she, her father and her brother died in quick succession, and

Račić Mausoleum

just as soon as the mausoleum was completed her mother followed them into it.

The mausoleum is one of the most important works by Croatia's most famous sculptor, Ivan Meštrović. The white-marble Byzantine sepulchre dates from 1922. Topped with a cupola and featuring sculpted angels, dogs and eagles, along with the four Račić sarcophagi, it's a quite extraordinary work. It excited mixed feelings in Rebecca West when she was here in 1937: 'There are some terrible errors, such as four boy musician angels, who recall the horrid Japaneseries of Aubrey Beardsley … but there are moments in the chapel which exquisitely illustrate the theory that the goodness of God stretches under human destiny, like the net below trapeze acts at the circus.'

If you're after something a little less esoteric, there's a pleasant walk around the headland, with plenty of places where you can swim off the rocks, and regular trips across the bay for 50 kuna to the tiny, almost barren island of **Supetar**, which boasts a simple restaurant.

If you want to stay in Cavtat there are lots of private rooms available (just ask around – or contact the tourist office on tel: 479 025; fax: 478 025). There are also

VLAHO BUKOVAC – VIRTUOSO PAINTER

Vlaho Bukovac was born in Cavtat in 1855, and showed prodigious talent from an early age. In 1877 he went to the Beaux-Arts in Paris to complete his studies and a year later became the first Croatian painter to be accepted into the prestigious Paris Salon. Travelling widely around Europe, Bukovac nonetheless played a vital part in the development of Croatian art – not just by being enormously prolific himself (he left over 2,000 works) but by supporting younger artists as well.

In his forties Bukovac spent five years living in Cavtat before accepting the

a number of hotels, including one of Croatia's largest, the stunning multi-tiered, 482-room, five-star **Hotel Croatia** (tel: 475 555; fax: 478 213; www.hoteli-croati.hr), which does sea-view doubles at around €200 in season, dropping back to €112 in winter. The hotel is happily sheltered from view by the headland, and has its own beaches (both standard and naturist). It's also home to the Feral restaurant, which has live music every evening.

Also run by the same management as the Croatia is the rather more endearing, if very traditional, stone-built **Hotel Supetar** (tel: 479 833; fax: 479 858), which has 28 three-star rooms right on the Cavtat quayside, with doubles priced very reasonably at €75 in summer and €46 in winter.

post of Professor of Fine Arts in Prague, though he returned to his childhood home regularly until shortly before his death in 1922.

At their best, Bukovac's paintings are simply marvellous, combining an almost photographic realism with impressionistic touches, and some of his portraits are truly stunning. As a virtuoso painter, he seems to have had a penchant for technically difficult or daring compositions, and there's a wonderful picture of a woman coming in (or going out?) through a doorway, which is in the Museum of Modern Art in Dubrovnik, along with a brilliant portrait of his daughter.

One of the best of the town's many restaurants is **Leut** (tel: 479 050), at the southern end of the town, right on the water. It's been in the Bobić family since 1971, and the food is excellent, as you'd expect for the price – though even an advance reservation won't necessarily guarantee they'll keep your waterside table here.

South to the Montenegrin border

Past the airport of the same name you'll find the pretty village of **Čilipi**. After Sunday mass the locals put on a show of folk music and dancing in the main square here, so it's not surprising that it's become something of a Sunday-morning excursion from Dubrovnik and the nearby resort hotels.

Three buses a day run from Dubrovnik to Čilipi and on to **Molunat**, a tiny fishing village in a lovely cove right at the very end of Croatia. With just a handful of private rooms, and no hotels nearby, it's within an hour of Dubrovnik, and an utterly charming place to stay. To be honest, however, given the bus times and the minuteness of the place, you'd need to be in Dubrovnik on an extended visit to make the excursion worthwhile.

THE ELAPHITE ISLANDS (KOLOČEP, LOPUD, ŠIPAN)

The Elaphite islands lie in a string north of Dubrovnik. Only three are now inhabited (Koločep, Lopud and Šipan), and these are connected by a ferry which runs up and down their length from Dubrovnik three times daily. The Elaphites make for a great excursion, getting you away from the crowds and into nature; there are no cars on Koločep and Lopud, and barely a handful on Šipan. If you're interested in staying in private rooms or apartments it's well worth contacting Elaphiti Travel (tel: 452 983; fax: 456 345; www.elaphiti.hr), which specialises in accommodation on the islands.

The first Elaphite island you'll see is **Daksa**, just 500m out of Dubrovnik's port, which may or may not still be for sale – the whole six-hectare island was being advertised at a cool US$3.5 million, including a large house, a ruined monastery, a boat-house and a dock through 2002 and 2003, but by 2004 it seemed to be off the market again. Either way, would your karma ever recover from buying a place where dozens of Dubrovnik intellectuals were massacred by the Partisans in 1944?

Beyond the city

Koločep

The first inhabited island in the Elaphites is Koločep, just 7km and 25 minutes away from Dubrovnik on the ferry, making it a very easy day trip. The ferry – which costs just 11 kuna – docks at Donje Čelo, and although there's another settlement on the other side of the island, it's here that you'll find the main infrastructure.

Outside the tourist season Koločep has an official population of just 148, and the doctor only comes once a week. Indeed, if you come here before May, you'll find only a single shop and a post office open in the mornings, and nowhere on the island to eat or drink at all – so bring a picnic, and make sure you know what time the last ferry leaves.

Donje Čelo is spread around a gentle bay, and has a biggish and reasonably sandy beach. A concrete path heads up from the ferry landing and winds across the island, leading through lovely woods and dry-stone-walled fields to the settlement of Gornje Čelo on Koločep's southeastern shore – where you'll find a couple of bars in summer and nothing whatsoever in winter. Smaller paths head on into the scented woods, and the island's sufficiently large for you to lose sight of anyone else, but small enough to avoid getting lost.

If you want to stay (from May to October), there's a single hotel in Donje Čelo, across the bay from the ferry landing, called the **Ville Koločep** (tel: 757 025; fax: 757 027). At the height of the season expect to pay €115 a night for doubles, including obligatory half board, in one of the eight buildings comprising the 150-room three-star hotel. In May and October the rate drops to €53 a night. When the hotel's open there are also three restaurants on the island, two near the ferry terminal and the other one beyond the hotel. There are also a handful of private rooms available – just ask on arrival if you haven't made prior arrangements.

Lopud

Half an hour – and a mere 8 kuna more on the ferry – beyond Koločep is the larger island of Lopud. Important in Ragusan times, it once had a population of 4,000 and harboured nearly 100 ships, as well as being home to Miho Pracat, the man whose bust sits in the Rector's Palace in Dubrovnik (see box, page 195).

Today the 4.5km-long island has a population of just 348 (though locals put the figure even lower, at barely half that). Everyone lives in one settlement, the eponymous Lopud, on a curved bay with a decent beach facing the village of Suđurađ on the next-door island of Šipan. There's no traffic, no pollution and no crime – and out of season nothing much open beyond a bar and a couple of shops. In summer, however, Lopud really comes into its own, and the village positively hums; it's a great place to come for the day or even for a holiday in its own right.

There's not a huge amount to see or do, but if you're here (and it's open) check out the church above the harbour, which has some fine 16th-century Venetian paintings and lovely 15th-century carved choir stalls. The church – one of 33 on the island – forms part of the Franciscan Monastery, which was dissolved by the French in 1808.

Also of interest is the small town museum and treasury, which are just off the quay opposite the end of the harbour, on Zlatarska. If they're closed – and they usually seem to be – pop through the gap between the two into a walled courtyard and seek out Lopud's priest, Don Ivan Vlašić, who holds the keys.

The treasury houses an assortment of ancient icons, vestments and sacred remnants, and a handful of very battered 9th-, 11th- and 12th-century frescos. In the museum you'll find an extraordinary and eclectic assembly of stuff ranging from Roman amphorae to 500-year-old pudding bowls to 19th-century English pottery. There's a nasty-looking French bayonet from 1806, a couple of pulleys from Miho Pracat's ship, and a cloak from the Giorgis, one of Dubrovnik's last noble families. Most curious of all is a shaving gown which belonged to King Charles V of Spain, which was a gift to **Miho Pracat** (see page 195). If you're coming just to see the gown, check it's back from the restorers, as that's where it was in summer 2004.

Behind the museum you can see the crumbling ruins of the Dubrovnik rector's summer palace, testimony to the fact that even now there are far more houses on Lopud than there are people. Walk further along the quayside, and there's a lovely park featuring tall pines and palms – each one planted, it's said, by grateful sailors who'd avoided shipwreck.

Just beyond the park, before the Grand Hotel, there's a path leading up to the left which crosses the island and comes out half an hour later at **Šunj**, one of the loveliest beaches on the Adriatic. On the crest of the hill, on the left, there's a concrete monument to **Viktor Dyk**, the Czech poet, author and political journalist, who died unexpectedly of a heart attack while on holiday here in May 1931, aged only 53.

The sandy beach at Šunj has a lovely shallow descent into the water and a temporary bar/restaurant open in season. It's an ill-kept secret, however, with sizeable crowds of locals coming over from the mainland on summer weekends.

The name Šunj provides the clue to Lopud's apparently mysterious use of a snake swallowing a child on its coat of arms – something you're more likely to have seen as the right half of the Alfa Romeo logo. According to the legend, Otto Visconti was shipwrecked here in 1098, on his way back from the crusades, and so grateful was he to survive that he had a votive church built on the hill above the bay. This was decorated with a copy of a shield which had been used by one of the defeated Saracens – featuring the snake and the child – and which subsequently became the Visconti crest. Over time the locale became known as *biscione*, the Italian for 'big snake', which was later abbreviated to Šunj.

The present church of Our Lady of Šunj (*Gospa od Šunja*) above the bay – turn left just after the Dyk memorial, if you're coming from Lopud – dates from the end of the 15th century. If it's open (which sadly is not all that often) it's well worth looking in to see the marvellous carved wooden altarpiece featuring Mary and the apostles. This, oddly enough, is English, from the 16th century. Lopud sailors – arguably among the best in the world at the time – heard that Henry VIII was in conflict with the pope and busily dissolving the monasteries, so off they went to go and buy relics and religious treasures while they were going cheap. The background to the altarpiece shows the Lopud ship which brought the Madonna here.

There's a direct path leading back from the church into the town; off to the right

MIHO PRACAT AND THE KING'S SHAVING GOWN

Born into a wealthy family on Lopud in 1528, Miho Pracat sought fame and fortune at sea but twice returned home penniless and in tatters. On the third try, however, he succeeded, and came back to Lopud a fabulously wealthy man – having saved Spain, it's said, from starvation after a bad harvest by using his ships to supply grain (no doubt at a healthy premium).

At an audience with a grateful King Charles V, Pracat was offered gold and a post as a colonial governor, but being wealthy and a patriotic Ragusan to boot he refused both. Instead, he asked for the king's shaving gown – which is why it's in Lopud's Town Museum today.

Pracat's only problem, it seems, was fertility – neither of his two wives produced an heir for him. When he finally died, in 1607, Pracat left his enormous fortune to the republic, mostly in the form of trusts. He was rewarded with the only statue ever raised to one of its own citizens – you can see it today in the Rector's Palace in Dubrovnik.

of this, heading away from Šunj, there's a track leading up to a great ruined fortress. Built originally in the 16th century, it was reinforced and expanded by the French from 1808 to 1813. Today it's soulful and dilapidated, and there's nothing special to see – though the views across to the island of Šipan are fabulous.

If you want to stay on Lopud there are quite a few **private rooms and apartments** for rent (ask on arrival, or contact Elaphiti Travel – see introductory section), as well as a single hotel, the three-star **Lafodia** (tel: 759 022; fax: 759 026), at the far end of the bay from the ferry terminal and harbour. There's a new swimming pool, and altogether there are some 200 rooms, with sea-view doubles with balconies going for €100, including the obligatory half board. In May and October that drops to €60; the hotel and most of the island's restaurants are closed from November to April.

By 2006, it seems likely that the Grand Hotel will have been restored to its former glories, 70 years after first opening its doors to grand tourists. It's set back from the seafront in what was once a lovely garden (and presumably will be again), and is a striking modernist curiosity, architecturally, having been the first concrete hotel to be built on the Adriatic.

There are restaurants and bars all along the front, but it's also worth climbing up the street near the harbour to Terrasse Peggy, which does a great grill in summer and boasts breezy views out across the sea to the island of Šipan. Try the local versions of *limoncello* and a curiously potent, nameless local drink made from honey and herbs.

Šipan

Furthest away, largest and least-visited of the Elaphites, Šipan is lovely. Known as the 'Golden Island', it once had 300,000 olive trees and a sizeable population, but centuries of emigration have left it with fewer than 500 inhabitants and – like Lopud – with many more houses than people. During Dubrovnik's Golden Age, it was fashionable for wealthy nobles to spend the summer season on Šipan, and you'll come across their (mostly dilapidated) summer residences all over the island – along with a smattering of Roman ruins and a score of churches from the 11th century onwards, but the main reason to come here is very much to get away from it all.

It takes the best part of two hours to get to Šipan from Dubrovnik (and costs a princely 14 kuna), with the ferry stopping at both the southwestern and northeastern ends. The main centres – and the only places where you'll find anything at all to eat or drink – are the ferry terminals: **Šipanska Luka**, to the northwest, at the end of a deep inlet, and **Suđurađ** to the southeast, opposite Lopud. The two settlements are about 7km apart, and connected by an irregular minibus. There's also a handful of other hamlets across the island.

An excellent excursion is to take the ferry to one end of the island and then walk across to the other end and catch the return ferry home from there. It takes a leisurely two hours by the most direct route, on Šipan's only paved road. The interior of the island is a fertile valley where you'll see grapes, figs and olives being grown, and there are plenty of places to stop and have a picnic and a bottle of wine.

You can also wander up any of the many tracks leading up to the island's two limestone ridges, where you'll find abandoned olive groves surrounded by crumbling dry-stone walls – though above Šipanska Luka itself work is progressing apace on bringing some of the olive trees back into production. You may also come across the rooting-marks made by wild boar here. They're a recent arrival on the island, and something of a nuisance to the olive farmers, having swum across from the mainland after a forest fire at the end of the 1990s.

As you traverse the island, look out for the ruined Napoleonic fortress on the southern ridge, along with a hospital and barracks dating from the same era. There are also secretive military tunnels which dive into the hillside nearby, though for the time being these are off limits to the public.

If you're walking from Šipanska Luka to Suđurađ you'll pass a great fortress of a church dating from the 16th century, dedicated to **Sveti Duh** (the Holy Spirit), as you climb up out of the central valley. Just after this the road forks – if you go right it passes the local clinic and loops down to the port; if you go straight on it goes directly through Suđurađ itself before emerging at the harbour.

The dominating feature of Suđurađ is the summer residence of Vice Stjepović-Skočibuha, which is the only one of Šipan's 42 original mansions to be entirely preserved. It was built in 1563, with the tower being added in 1577, and is today used for conferences and functions. It houses an excellent restaurant and bar, Na Taraci, which is about the only place you'll find anything to eat at this end of the island.

If you want to explore further afield, you'll find boats down on the harbour whose owners are happy to take you out to the uninhabited Elaphite islands as well as to delightful unspoiled coves and beaches on Šipan itself – if there's nobody around ask at the little bar along the harbour front, which is where most of the fishermen and seafaring types hang out.

There's only one **hotel** on the island, the two-star Šipan (tel: 758 000; fax: 758 003), which is in a great location on Šipanska Luka's harbour. There are 80 fairly functional rooms, with sea-view doubles going for €86 a night at the height of the season, dropping to €48 in May and October. Everything on the island is pretty much closed from November to April. There's also a handful of **private rooms** at both ends of the island, and you may find people touting these as you get off the boat – otherwise just ask around.

MLJET

Mljet is one of the most attractive islands in the whole Adriatic. Despite being unusually beautiful, and entirely unspoiled by deforestation (it was never ruled by Venice, hence also the lack of towns of any size), it has hitherto remained relatively unvisited – though with the new, fast connection from Dubrovnik more people are coming every year. Nonetheless, the island is easily big enough, at over 100km², to absorb many more visitors without getting overcrowded.

The entire western end of Mljet is a national park, and features two gorgeous salt-water lakes, the larger of which has an island with a ruined monastery on it. It's easy to visit on a day trip from Dubrovnik, but if you want to stay longer there's a hotel and some private rooms, and the island has great walking, cycling and canoeing, along with a nascent (if rather casual) diving school, and the opportunity of learning to sail.

Legend has it that Ulysses stopped here for seven years on his Odyssey, and while there's absolutely no historical basis for the assertion, it makes a nice story.

More credence can be given to the theory that on his way to martyrdom in Rome, St Paul was shipwrecked here, not on Malta. It's not just the name (Mljet used to be called Melita), but also the snakes – St Paul was bitten by one soon after arriving, which would be improbable (then as now) on Malta, whereas Mljet was notoriously snake-infested until the last century.

Less speculative is the island's use by the Illyrians and the Romans – the remains of the Illyrian fort can still be seen on the summit of Mali Gradac, near **Babine Kuče**, while the settlement of **Polače** is named after the ruins of the 4th- or 5th-century Roman palace there.

The next significant development was in 1151, when Mljet was given to the Benedictines, who built the monastery on St Mary's Island. They stayed on even though Mljet itself was handed over to Dubrovnik in 1333, and lived a peaceful life until the arrival of Napoleon's troops in 1808, after which the monastery was abandoned.

The administrative centre of the island, **Babino Polje**, dates from the Middle Ages, but apart from the monastery, nothing on the western end of the island reaches back beyond the late 18th century, and the new port of **Pomena** wasn't established until after World War II.

Wildlife

Mljet is famous for being the only place in Europe where you can find mongooses in the wild. The Indian grey mongoose was introduced to Mljet in 1910, by the

Austrians, in an attempt to eradicate the infestation of venomous snakes. This had been a problem since time immemorial – and was probably the reason why the Benedictines built their monastery on the island in the first place ('Never mind the beauty and the isolation, Brother Jacob, let's get away from those blasted snakes!').

Seven male and four female mongooses were introduced, and they adapted well to the Mljet lifestyle, proliferating and practically eradicating the snake population over the next 20 years. So successful were they, in fact, that they lost their statutory protection in 1949, and excessive numbers have proven difficult to curb. Small animals, as well as both resident and migratory birds, fall prey to the feral hunters, and they're not over-popular with the islanders, either.

Mljet's other fauna used to include the Mediterranean monk seal, though none has been spotted here since 1974. You may however see the Turkish gecko, the sharp-snouted lizard, or Dahl's whip snake (if the mongooses haven't got to him first), and there are now quite a few fallow deer in the forests – following their introduction here in 1958.

Getting there

There's a daily Jadrolinija ferry from Dubrovnik, though as this arrives in Mljet in the afternoon and returns at 06.00 in the morning it does mean an overnight stopover. The crossing takes around four hours. In summer, however, you can take the one-and-a-half-hour crossing on the fast catamaran, *Nona Ana*, which comes out to Mljet in the morning and returns in the afternoon. The fare is around 50 kuna

Pelješac

Kanal

Tristenik

Catamaran

Pomena

Hotel Odisej

Mali Most

Goveđari

Polače

Sobra Dubrovnik

Malo Jezero

Babine Kuče

Veliko Jezero

Sv Marija

Pristanište

Soline

Mljet National Park

N

Bradt

0 _____ 5km
0 _____ 3mls

Catamaran

Sobra

Post office

Petrol

Ferry & catamaran

Prožura

Maranovići

Korita

Saplunara

Dubrovnik

return. It is also possible to go direct from Bari to Mljet as the Jadrolinija ferry to Dubrovnik stops at Sobra three times a week.

All ferries dock just east of **Sobra**, about a third of the way along Mljet's north shore, and are met by the local bus – but be warned that on busy days in summer there can be fewer buses than passengers, and if you're stranded your only realistic option is to rent a bike – at sellers' prices (and it's a long, hard, hot and hilly ride). To solve this problem the catamaran has taken to sailing on to **Polače**, and if you're on a day trip this is definitely the way to go. There's also an SEM ferry linking Polače with Trstenik on the Pelješac peninsula between mid July and mid September.

The easiest way of seeing Mljet is by taking an all-inclusive package from Dubrovnik (available from all the usual agencies – see page 76). These go for around 200–300 kuna and include the ferry fare, a trip out to the island on the lake, and a guided tour, as well as the chance to swim. Bring a bottle of wine and a picnic, and it makes a wonderful day out.

Getting around

Apart from the local buses that run between Sobra and Pomena to coincide with the Jadrolinija ferry arrivals and departures, there's no public transport.

If you want to cycle on the island the best place to rent bikes is at the Hotel Odisej, in Pomena, or by the lakes themselves. Rates run from 20 kuna an hour to 110 kuna a day, and the paths around the lakes are absolutely perfect for cyclists. (There are several other places which rent out bikes too, if the stock at the Odisej's already out on loan, or if you haven't yet got as far as Pomena, including Sobra and Polače.) Even on the main roads, there's no traffic to speak of. You can rent buggies or cars and scooters outside the hotel, too, as well as at Sobra and Polače, with cars going from around 400 kuna a day, including fuel and 100km.

Where to stay and eat

The monastery on St Mary's Island served from 1960 to 1988 as the lovely Hotel Melita, but since it was handed back to the Dubrovnik bishopric it's fallen into ruin. Although restoration commenced in 2004, nobody's sure what will become of it – there's no doubt it would make the most wonderful boutique hotel, but there are also plans to turn it into a research or information centre, or to leave it as a visitor attraction. At present, there's just a restaurant serving the numerous visitors to the island throughout the day.

For the time being, therefore, Mljet has only one hotel, the three-star **Odisej** (tel: 020 744 022; fax: 020 744 042; www.hotelodisej.hr), in Pomena, which has 150 rooms spread across a number of buildings, with sea-view doubles with balconies going for around €140 a night at the peak of the season, and €80 outside July and August. The hotel shuts down from November until just before Easter.

Mljet also has a reasonable (and steadily increasing) supply of **private rooms**, but it's often essential to book ahead. This can be arranged through the Mini Brum tourist agency in Babino Polje (tel: 098 285 566; fax: 020 745 260). For rooms outside the national park, you can also try the rather intermittent tourist office in

Babino Polje (tel/fax: 020 745 125) or – within the park itself – that in Goveđari (tel: 020 744 086; fax: 020 744 186; email: tz-mjesta@du.htnet.hr). Polače, a few kilometres away from the Hotel Odisej, but still within easy walking distance of the lakes, has excellent private rooms on the shore, and also has a bakery and a couple of cheerful restaurants. Pomena, too, has some good private accommodation, including the highly recommended Apartments Stražičić (tel/fax: 20 41 91 22; email: slavica.strazicic@du.htnet.hr), where a double apartment costs 450 kuna a night in July and August, or 340 kuna at other times. Half-a-dozen restaurants line the harbour, which is very popular with visiting yachtsmen (as indeed is Polače), but food shopping is limited to the early-morning bakery van, a couple of fruit stalls and the absolute basics.

There are two basic **campsites** on the island – one in Babino Polje, the other in Ropa. Other, more personal sites are run by private individuals – just ask around when you arrive at the port.

Activities

If you're here for more than a day trip, take advantage of the island's excellent **walking and hiking**. From the gentle paths around the lakes to the harder trails into the hills, Mljet's unspoiled beauty is overwhelming, and away from the lakes you'll pretty much have the place to yourself. Even on the lakeshore, you don't have to walk far to have almost total seclusion. There's a good marked trail from near Soline up Montokuč overlooking the lakes (the ascent takes around 40 minutes), with great views from the top. Rather than retrace your steps, you could return to Pristanište or continue to Polače or Goveđari. Within the park, trails lead to unexplored coves on the island's northwest tip, while even outside the park the ratio of nature to people is very high.

If it's **watersports** you're after, there's plenty of choice. Exploring by **kayak or canoe** makes for a great way of seeing the lakes at your own pace – they can be rented by the little bridge or at the hotel, with prices roughly the same as for bikes (see page 204). Windsurfers can be rented out from the hotel, too, and there's also a sailing school based here, though it's a pity they don't have dinghies on hand. For divers, the local diving centre (book through the hotel or phone Mario on 098 479 916) can take you out to a Roman wreck, complete with original amphorae, or to a defunct German U-boat. Expect to pay €43 for a dive with a guide, including equipment – though if you're a novice you might want to take heed of reports of a certain laxity in this department. Visits to either of the wrecks cost an additional €10.

What to see
Mljet National Park

Mljet's main draw is the national park, and specifically the two salt-water lakes, **Veliko Jezero** (with St Mary's Island and the ruins of the monastery) St Mary's Mljet Monastery and **Malo Jezero** – literally 'Big Lake' and 'Small Lake'. If you're on a day trip you won't have time to see a great deal else.

St Mary's Monastery, Mljet

As you'll probably guess – the salt water's a bit of a giveaway – neither Malo nor Veliko Jezero is actually a lake. The sea feeds into the larger one, and that feeds into the smaller one. The tidal changes allowed the monks to run a useful watermill in the past, and although the mill's long gone you can still easily see which way the tide's headed from the bridge over the shallow channel between Malo and Veliko Jezero.

Unfortunately the bridge originally spanning the seaward exit of Veliko Jezero was lost when the channel was widened and deepened in 1960, so you can't now do the full 12km circuit round the lake without getting wet. *A word of warning*: If you decide to swim the 13.6m wide and 2.6m deep channel, be very sure which way the current's going, and how fast it's moving – there's an awful lot of water coming in and out of here, and it's frighteningly easy to be swept out to sea.

The boat out to **St Mary's Island** (Sveti Marija) runs several times a day, and the fare is included in the national park entry fee. On the island itself there's not been much to see in recent years, but the monastery is currently being restored and the church is now open for services at 11.30 on Sunday. You can visit the monks' gardens, complete with lemon trees, in the original cloisters (if they're open). The island also has a couple of restaurants, which are highly popular as the luncheon venues for excursions, as well as ice-cream stopovers.

Take the ten-minute path around the little island and you'll see two other plain but evocative votive chapels dating from the 17th or 18th century. These were built by grateful sailors who'd survived shipwrecks or storms. If you're here in spring, you'll find lots of wild asparagus, while in summer you'll be overwhelmed by the noise of cicadas in the afternoon haze.

Established in 1960, the national park (tel: 020 744 041; fax: 020 744 043; www.np-mljet.hr) is run from the settlement of **Govedari**, roughly equidistant from both Pomena and Polače. Entry is 65 kuna, and the money goes to the upkeep of the park, so don't be tempted to try and avoid paying. Anyway, if you're caught without a ticket, you'll be charged – double. Detailed maps are available from the park office (on the shore of the main lake, at the locality called **Pristanište**) or from the kiosk selling tickets in Pomena, though the footpath network shown on these maps is none too accurate. There's another kiosk on the road in from Polače.

The national park is unusual among nature reserves in including the main villages, the hotel and the basic tourist infrastructure within its boundaries, but don't be lulled into a sense of false security. You're in an ecologically fragile area here, and it's important to follow the rules, especially relating to fire – in 1917 an accidental blaze destroyed much of the old forest and the restoration took decades. So don't light fires, don't smoke, don't camp – and do stay on the paths.

Beyond the national park

Three-quarters of Mljet is forest-covered, meaning good shade in the summer heat (but take plenty of water with you; there are no supplies at all), while the few settlements are rarely visited, and you'll be made to feel welcome by the locals. This is especially true on the 15km stretch of the island east of Sobra, where the settlements of **Prožura**, **Maranovići** and **Korita** are practically never visited by foreigners. Right at the far eastern tip, at Sapunara, are two sandy beaches, the only ones on the island. You'll need a car (or a bike, and strong legs) to get here as no buses run beyond Sobra. The first is below the village itself; the other, round the next bay, has a shallow and very sheltered lagoon, and is almost deserted. Debris washed in on the tide is a problem in parts at present, but with the current promotion by the tourist board, this – and the seclusion – are likely to change.

The highest point on the island (Veli Grad, 513m) is just above Mljet's diminutive administrative capital, **Babino Polje**, which sits on the side of the island's largest field system – the endless dry-stone walls here are the result of centuries of clearing stones from the fields. The main produce is olives and (surprisingly expensive but incredibly tasty) goat's cheese. Much of the island's very drinkable wine comes from the village of **Blato**, just outside the national park.

Once the new bypass is open, the capital is likely to be even less visited by tourists.

Directly south of Babino Polje is **Ulysses Cave** (Odisejeva spilja), a good half-hour's tough walk across fields and down the cliff, but well worth the effort – though not suitable for young children. Also visited on a boat trip from Odisej Hotel, it's a magical cave to explore in calm seas.

TRSTENO

Just 18km up the coast from Dubrovnik is the little village of Trsteno, which would be entirely unremarkable were it not for the wonderful arboretum here. Originally created as the summer residence and gardens of Ivan Gučetić, a Dubrovnik noble, in 1502, and expanded over the centuries, the estate was nationalised by the communists in 1948 and re-branded as the Arboretum of the Yugoslav (now Croatian) Academy of Arts and Sciences.

The gardens here are delightful, and make a charming excursion out of Dubrovnik. The bus to Split, which goes every half-hour or so, sets down and picks up in the middle of the village, where the first thing you'll see is a splendid pair of huge 500-year-old plane trees. Beyond these, heading towards the sea in a series of terraces, is the arboretum itself (open 08.00–15.00 daily in winter; until 20.00 in summer; entry 15 kuna).

There's nothing special to do other than to wander round the gardens, which vary from the formality of the oldest part, beneath the villa, with geometrical box hedges enclosing different planted areas, to the wilder areas off to the sides. There's a lovely orchard with citrus fruits, avenues of palms and firs, and all manner of exotic semi-tropical plants, most of them usefully labelled. There's even a rather fanciful 18th-century grotto, where you'll find Neptune with his trident presiding over a water-lily-strewn fishpond and playful water-spouting fountains in the form of dolphins.

STON AND THE PELJEŠAC PENINSULA

Thirty kilometres beyond Trsteno, and under 50km from Dubrovnik, is the town of Ston – or rather the towns of Ston, as it's divided into Mali Ston on the north coast, and Veliki Ston on the south coast, across the isthmus of the Pelješac peninsula.

The reason for a visit here is twofold – firstly to see (and clamber upon) a set of defensive walls which rival Dubrovnik's own, and secondly to sample Croatia's best oysters and mussels, which are farmed here. The walls were built from the 14th century on, primarily to protect the salt-pans – the salt trade was one of the republic's biggest earners, and it's said that Napoleon was even more keen to get his hands on Ston than Dubrovnik. Today 20 of the original 40 towers and some 5km of walls are still standing, and if you climb high enough up – the public access is from Veliki Ston – there are great views across to the island of Mljet (see page 199).

The area was badly hit by an earthquake in 1996, which destroyed many of the houses in both Veliki and Mali Ston, along with most of the town of Slano, further down the coast towards Dubrovnik – and even today many of the properties here remain boarded up. Nonetheless, Mali Ston's tourist infrastructure is thriving, and the village is increasingly popular with Dubrovnik romantics.

The easiest way to get to Ston is on one of the buses heading up the Pelješac peninsula to Orebić or Trpanj; if one of the three buses a day in this direction isn't convenient then an alternative is the half-hourly or so bus to Split, which sets down at the junction on the main road. This is only a 15-minute walk from Mali Ston; from here it's a further 15 minutes on to Veliki Ston.

If you decide to stay over, there are two lovely small hotels in Mali Ston. Just outside the old walls is the attractive **Villa Koruna** (tel: 754 359; fax: 754 642) which has half a dozen simple doubles at €80 a night year-round, and a great covered terrace of a dining room, right on the water. Oysters go for 6 kuna a pop, while a plate of mussels comes in at 25 kuna. The lobster (at an eye-watering 400 kuna a kilo) is superb. Just inside the walls is the somewhat more upmarket **Ostrea** (tel: 754 555; fax: 754 575), which has nine rooms at €150 a night. The tourist office in Veliki Ston (tel/fax: 754 452) can point you in the direction of the few private rooms available locally. There are also two great restaurants on the harbour in Mali Ston, the Kapetanova Kuča and the Taverna Bota.

To explore the villages, vineyards and coves of the rugged 65km-long Pelješac peninsula, along with the lovely town and island of Korčula, which it leads to, you'll need more time and probably your own set of wheels – and of course the excellent *Croatia: The Bradt Travel Guide*.

THE NERETVA DELTA

Further still up the mainland coast, beyond Bosnia's sea corridor at Neum, is the last piece of land in Dubrovnik County, the extraordinary Neretva Delta.

Long a marshy, malarial swamp, the pancake-flat river delta is now a series of fertile agricultural wetlands, producing Croatia's best citrus fruits (you'll see delicious tangerines for sale along the roadside), and providing shelter to waterfowl and wading birds, as well as spawning grounds for many species of fish, including eels.

Deep in the delta are six hard-to-find dedicated ornithological reserves. You'll need time, patience, and your own transport – in which case you should keep a weather-eye on the main road for flying customs squads, on the lookout for Bosnian contraband and speeding tourists.

A total of 299 species of bird have been recorded in the delta, with 92 nesting here, including the pigmy cormorant, coots, crakes, warblers and shrikes, several species of heron and egret, all five species of European grebe and almost every species of European duck. In 1999, a government proposal was initiated to proclaim the entire delta as a nature park, but obstacles include various development and road-improvement plans.

Easily the best way of visiting is to persuade one of the locals to take you around in a punt (the indigenous *trupica*), poling you along the reedy channels which separate the reclaimed market gardens, and giving you a chance to soak up the mysterious atmosphere. Far simpler is to book yourself on a day-long excursion from Dubrovnik for around 300 kuna – this includes a comprehensively guided boat tour and is available from most local travel agencies. Take insect repellent with you – the mosquitoes here can be fearsome.

BOSNIA & HERZEGOVINA

If you're in Dubrovnik for a week or so you might consider a trip into next-door Bosnia & Herzegovina. There are three obvious destinations – Trebinje, which is just 30km north of Dubrovnik; Mostar, which requires a full day trip; and Medjugorje, a must for millions of religious pilgrims. Each of the three is easiest to reach on one of the many excursions offered by Dubrovnik's travel agents.

Trebinje

Trebinje is just across the border from Dubrovnik and is the southernmost town in Herzegovina. It's been famous forever for its Saturday market, although as you'd expect mass tourism has taken its toll, and you should no longer expect to experience the truly authentic Turkish-style market or see the peasant costumes of bygone eras. That said, Trebinje is a pretty stone-built town surrounded by stark mountains, and it's well worth a wander around. There's also a spectacular steep stone bridge over the Trebisnjica River which dates back to Ottoman times, a 15th-century Orthodox monastery, and a clutch of small mosques.

Mostar

For centuries, Mostar was to most people its old bridge, spanning the Neretva River – which was hardly surprising, as *most* means bridge and *stari* means old. The elegant single-span structure featured an arch 20m high and 30m wide, and was completed by the Turks in 1557. The architect, who had been threatened with death if the bridge collapsed, dug his own grave shortly before completion, but fled before the final unveiling.

The bridge, of course, was famously shelled to destruction in the recent war (by the Croatians), but was painstakingly rebuilt and finally completed in 2004 – you'd hardly know it from the original. Hopefully the new bridge (should they change the town name to Novimost?) will help reunite the communities on either side of the river, though at the time of writing that dream looked some way from being fulfilled.

Visitors come to Mostar for a flavour of East-meets-West, and the town does have a cheerful bazaar (where the unwary can find recently made antiques) and several interesting mosques. You can even have a dip in the marvellously unrestored Austro-Hungarian public baths, if you're feeling brave.

Bear in mind that Mostar makes for a long day out from Dubrovnik – the round trip covers the best part of 300km, on mostly winding roads.

Medjugorje

Nestled up in the Bosnian hills, between the coast and Mostar, the small village of Medjugorje was entirely unknown to the outside world until the Virgin Mary appeared to half a dozen local teenagers there on June 24 1981. Since then, more than 15 million pilgrims have visited the site, and there's now a vast infrastructure in place to take care of them. If you're a pilgrim, then the visit is an absolute must (indeed Dubrovnik will probably take second place); if not, you may find the whole affair rather baffling. Either way, you should read up about it – there are thousands of websites – before you go.

Pomegranates

MONTENEGRO

If you have the time it's also well worth considering a side-trip to Montenegro, which starts just 40km south of Dubrovnik. The obvious nearby attractions here are the extraordinary Bay of Kotor and the country's diminutive former capital, Cetinje. Several of the travel agencies in Dubrovnik offer a full-day tour including both.

The Bay of Kotor

The Bay of Kotor is a vast natural harbour which is the nearest thing the Mediterranean has to a fjord, with the town of Kotor itself being 30km from the open sea. The harbour allowed for the development of unparalleled maritime skills in the Middle Ages, which evolved naturally into piracy by the 15th century and

later gave the seas internationally renowned navigators and naval engineers. The bay is surrounded by steep grey mountains which plunge into the sea, and is dominated by the bulk of Mount Lovčen (1,749m).

The road from Dubrovnik winds its way around the bay passing through the resorts of **Hercog Novi**, **Kamenari** and **Risan** before reaching the charming Venetian-inspired town of **Perast**. Out in the bay are a couple of delightful islands with monasteries which seem to slide attractively past as the bus winds its way along the coastline.

Some 15km further round the bay is **Kotor** itself, which was devastated in the 1979 earthquake but has since been much restored. It's a charming place, with narrow alleys and numberless little squares. Above the town are huge walls, twice the length of Dubrovnik's, which culminate in the impressively ruined Fortress of St John – though it's unlikely on an excursion that you'll have the time to make the two-hour walk up there and back.

Cetinje

High up in the Montenegrin hills, at 660m, and reached by a frankly terrifying road, is the small town of Cetinje. It must have been one of the world's most curious capitals. At its largest it had a population of only 15,000, and until under a century ago the only access was via a mule track – yet it boasted 15 foreign legations from some of the world's most powerful nations.

Cetinje became the capital of Montenegro in the 15th century, and it flourished rapidly – by 1493 it had the first printing press in the Balkans, and you can still see the first Bible printed here, barely a decade after Caxton.

Today the place has something of a museum feel to it, though the legations – abandoned during World War I – still have a distinctively national air to them (the British one wouldn't look out of place in Surrey). The fascinating town museum is housed in King Nikola I's palace, and contains pictures of most of Europe's royalty of the era, since the Montenegrin king successfully married off all eight of his daughters into European royal families. Unfortunately that was about the best thing he ever did – everything else we know about Nikola shows him up as a complete rotter, who thought nothing of betraying his country and people.

Quite a contrast, indeed, to the residents of the more homely **Biljarda Palace**, across the square (so-called because there was a billiard table here – a hell of a thing to have to carry up on a mule). The Biljarda was the residence of Montenegro's Prince Bishops, who ruled the country in the 18th and 19th centuries. The most famous – and still a hero to many Montenegrins today – was **Prince Petar II Petrović Njegoš**, who was a brilliant fighter, a great poet and an able diplomat. He entertained rare visitors to Cetinje by shooting lemons out of the air, but unfortunately caught tuberculosis and died at the age of 37 – ludicrously young for a Montenegrin. Njegoš is buried in a spectacular and hard-to-reach mausoleum, near the top of Mount Lovčen, 24km out of town, where you'll find a great granite sculpture of the famed Prince Bishop by Ivan Meštrović.

Language

Dubrovnik's official language is Croatian, written using a Latin alphabet. For 98.5% of the population, this is their mother tongue.

Croatian is a tough language to learn, but words are nothing like as difficult to pronounce as you'd think, since every letter always has a unique pronunciation – albeit not always the same as in English. Although you're unlikely to have time to learn much Croatian, grab at least a handful of words and phrases to take with you – the effort will be richly rewarded.

The Croatian language comes from the group described by linguists as Serbo-Croat, meaning that Serbs, Croats and Bosnians can readily understand each other – not that you'd necessarily know this, judging by the strife of the past 20 (or even 2,000) years. Within Croatia itself there are also regional variations and dialects, with the one you'll most likely notice being the three different ways Croats have of saying 'what?' The official version – used in the media – is the Slavonian 'Što?', but in the capital you'll hear 'kaj?' and along the coast it's invariably 'ča?'

The use of the Latin alphabet is largely to do with religion, and the east–west division of the Roman Empire – it was in Croatia in the 9th century that Saints Cyril and Methodius invented the Glagolitic alphabet, which was converted by St Clement, in Ohrid (now in the Former Yugoslav Republic of Macedonia), into the Cyrillic alphabet, variants of which are now used throughout the Orthodox world.

You probably won't see Cyrillic at all – unless you visit the Icon Museum or venture into neighbouring Bosnia or Montenegro.

Most people in Dubrovnik speak at least one foreign language, and English is widely understood.

PRONUNCIATION

Croatian words aren't anything like as hard to pronounce as you might expect them to be – just concentrate on pronouncing each letter the same way every time, and you won't go far wrong.

A	as in party
B	as in bed
C	as in fats, bats
Č, č	as in nurture, culture
Ć, ć	as in chew, chump
D	as in dote
Đ, đ	as in George, jam (sometimes written Dj, dj, to help non-natives – so you see both Tuđman and Tudjman written)
E	as in pet
F	as in free
G	as in goat
H	as in hat

I	as in **fee**t
J	as in **y**et
K	as in **k**ept
L	as in **l**eg
M	as in **m**other
N	as in **n**o
O	as in h**o**t
P	as in **p**ie
R	as in ai**r**
S	as in **s**and
Š, š	as in **sh**ovel
T	as in **t**oo
U	as in l**oo**k
V	as in **v**ery
Z	as in **z**oo
Ž, ž	as in trea**s**ure

WORDS AND PHRASES
Courtesies

hello/bye (informal)	*zdravo/bok*	good day	*dobar dan*
cheers!	*živjeli!*	good evening	*dobro večer*
good morning	*dobro jutro*	good night (on leaving)	*laku noć*

Language

how are you?	*kako ste*	thank you very much	*hvala lijepo*
I'm fine, thank you	*dobro, hvala*	excuse me	*izvinite*
please/thank you	*molim/hvala*	goodbye	*doviđenja*

Basic words

yes/no	*da/ne (nema = emphatic no)*	more/less	*više/manje*
		good/bad	*dobro/loše*
that's right	*tako je*	hot/cold	*toplo/hladno*
OK	OK	toilet	*zahod (also toalet)*
maybe	*možda*		
large/small	*veliko/malo*	men/women	*muški/ženski*

Numbers

1	*jedan*	9	*devet*
2	*dva*	10	*deset*
3	*tri*	12	*dvanaest*
4	*četiri*	15	*petnaest*
5	*pet*	20	*dvadeset*
6	*šest*	50	*pedeset*
7	*sedam*	100	*stotina*
8	*osam*	1,000	*hiljada*

Questions

How?	*Kako?*	Where?	*Gdje?*
How much?	*Koliko?*	Who?	*Tko?*
What's your name?	*Kako se zovete?*	Why?	*Zašto?*
When?	*Kada?*		

Do you speak English?	*Govorite li engleski?*
How do you say in Croatian?	*Kako se to kaže na hrvatskom?*
Can you tell me the way to...?	*Možete mi reči put do...?*
How do I get to...?	*Kako mogu doći do...?*
Is this the right way to...?	*Je li ovo pravi put do...?*
Is it far to walk?	*Je li daleko pješice?*
Can you show me on the map?	*Možete mi pokazati na karti?*

Shopping

bank	*banka*	market	*dućan/tržnica/ market*
bookshop	*knjižara*		
chemist	*ljekarna/apoteka*	money	*novac*
shop	*dućan*		

Post

post office	*pošta*	postcard	*razglednica*
letter	*pismo*	paper	*papir*
envelope	*omotnica*	stamp	*poštanska marka*

Language

Getting around

bus/bus station	*autobus/ autobusni kolodvor*	left/right	*lijevo/desno*
		straight on	*ravno*
plane/airport	*avion/aerodrom*	ahead/behind	*naprijed/iza*
car/taxi	*auto/taxi*	up/down	*gore/dolje*
petrol/petrol station	*benzin/benzinska stanica*	under/over	*ispod/preko*
		north/south	*sjever/jug*
entrance/exit	*ulaz/izlaz*	east/west	*istok/zapad*
arrival/departure	*dolazak/odlazak*	road/bridge	*cesta/most*
open/closed	*otvoreno/zatvoreno*	hill/mountain	*brežuljak/planina*
here/there	*ovdje/tamo*	village/town	*selo/grad*
near/far	*blizu/daleko*	waterfall	*slap*

Hotel

bed	*krevet*	toilet/wc	*zahod/wc* (pronounced 'vay-say')
room	*soba*		
key	*ključ*		
shower/bath	*tuš/kada*	hot water/cold water	*topla voda/ hladna voda*

Words and phrases

Miscellaneous

tourist office	*turistički ured*	dentist	*zubar*
consulate	*konzularni ured*	hospital/clinic	*bolnica/klinika*
doctor	*liječnik/doktor*	police	*policija*

Time

hour/minute	*sat/minuta*	yesterday	*jučer*
week/day	*tjedan/dan*	this week/next week	*ovaj tjedan/*
year/month	*godina/mjesec*		*slijedeći tjedan*
now	*sada*	morning/afternoon	*jutro/*
soon	*uskoro*		*poslije podne*
today/tomorrow	*danas/sutra*	evening/night	*večer/noć*
Monday	*ponedjeljak*	Friday	*petak*
Tuesday	*utorak*	Saturday	*subota*
Wednesday	*srijeda*	Sunday	*nedjela*
Thursday	*četvrtak*		
January	*siječanj*	July	*srpanj*
February	*veljača*	August	*kolovoz*
March	*ožujak*	September	*rujan*
April	*travanj*	October	*listopad*
May	*svibanj*	November	*studeni*
June	*lipanj*	December	*prosinac*

Language

| spring | *proljeće* | autumn | *jesen* |
| summer | *ljeto* | winter | *zima* |

Food and drink
Essentials

breakfast	*doručak*	hot	*vruće*
lunch	*ručak*	bread	*kruh*
dinner	*večera*	jam	*džem (some say*
water	*voda*		*pekmez)*
beer	*pivo*	coffee	*kava*
wine	*vino*	tea	*čaj*
white wine	*bijelo vino*	tea with milk*	*crni čaj su*
red wine	*crno vino*		*mlijekom*
rosé wine	*roze vino*	tea with lemon	*čaj su limunom*
house wine	*domaće vino*	sugar	*šećer*
spirit (generic)	*rakija*	salt	*slan*
spirit (from herbs)	*travarica*	cheese	*sir*
brandy	*lozovača*	soup	*juha*
pear spirit	*kruškovača*	thick soup	*ragu*
cold	*hladno*	egg (eggs)	*jaje (jaja)*

* ask for black, otherwise you get fruit tea with milk…

Words and phrases

ham	*šunka*	home-made	*domaće*
air-dried ham	*pršut*	grilled	*sa roštilja*
fish	*riba*	baked	*pečeno*
chips	*pomfrit*	fried	*prženo*
meat	*meso*	boiled	*kuhano*
vegetables	*povrće*	stuffed	*punjeno*
fruits	*voće*		

Fish

sardines	*sardina*	salmon trout	*losos*
mackerel	*skuša*	perch	*grgeč, smuđ*
bass	*luben*	squid	*lignje*
grey mullet	*cipal*	mussels	*školjka*
red mullet	*barbun*	oysters	*oštrige/kamenice*
bream	*zubatac*	crayfish	*škampi*
tuna	*tuna*	crab	*rak*
trout	*pastrva*	lobster	*jastog*

Meat

beef	*govedina*	mutton	*ovčetina*
pork	*svinjetina*	veal	*teletina*
lamb	*janjetina*	chicken	*piletina*

Language

Vegetables

potatoes	*krumpir*	onion	*luk*
rice	*riža*	garlic	*češnjak*
green peppers	*paprike*		

Salads

cucumber	*krastavac*	mixed	*miješana*
cabbage	*kupus*	with chillis and cheese	*grčka*
tomato	*rajčica* (or *paradajz*)	with tomatoes and	*šopska* (or *grčka*)
lettuce	*zelena*	cheese	

Fruit

orange	*narandža* (or *naranča*)	melon	*dinja*
lemon	*limun*	pears	*kruške*
plums	*šljive*	peaches	*breskve*

Further Information

BOOKS

Many of the books listed here are long out of print, but most can be found secondhand – either by trawling through old bookshops, or online at places like Abe Books (www.abebooks.com).

Beretić, Dubravka *Art Treasures of Dubrovnik* Jugoslavija Guides, 1968. Obscure guide dating back to the communist heyday – still remarkably accurate, however.

Coyler, William *Dubrovnik and the Southern Adriatic Coast from Split to Kotor* Ward Lock & Co, 1967. Delightfully dated mini-hardback with lots of black-and-white photos.

Goldstein, Ivo *Croatia: A History* C Hurst & Co, 1999 (2nd edition). Well-balanced Croat historian's view of Croatian history from Roman times to the present day. Hard to find, in spite of its relatively recent publication.

Harris, Robin *Dubrovnik – A History* Saqi, 2003. Solid doorstop of a hardback with a wealth of fascinating insight and wonderful illustrations – but quite a dent in the wallet at 25 quid.

Kaplan, Robert *Balkan Ghosts* Picador, 1994 (out of print). The author uses his 1990 odyssey through the Balkans to explain the conflictual politics across the region in depth. Relatively easily available secondhand.

Kastrapeli et al. *Dubrovnik Tourist Guide* Minčeta, 1967. Classic 1960s mini-guide – gushing prose, black-and-white photos.

Letcher, Piers *Croatia: The Bradt Travel Guide* Bradt, 2005 (2nd edition). Just the guide you need if you're going beyond the confines of this particular publication.

Margaritoni, Marko *Dubrovnik, Between History and Legend* Dubrovnik State Archives, 2001. Lots of wonderful tales and legends by a local author. Order the book for 200 kuna from the man himself, at marko.margaritoni@du.htnet.hr.

Murphy, Dervla *Through the Embers of Chaos – Balkan Journeys* John Murray, 2002. Brilliant account of a long cycle-tour through the Balkans, including Dubrovnik. Truly a wonderful, inspirational book.

Pavičić, Liliana and Pirker-Mosher, Gordana *The Best of Croatian Cooking* Hippocrene, 2000. You're back home and missing those Croatian dishes? This is the book for you.

Rellie, Annalisa *Montenegro: The Bradt Travel Guide* Bradt, 2003. Essential reading if you're digging deeper into Montenegro than we have been able to here.

Rheubottom, David *Age, Marriage and Politics in 15th-century Ragusa* Oxford University Press, 2000. Intriguing – if at times weighty – insights into the inter-relationships between politics, kinship and marriage in the republic. Expensive, however, even secondhand.

Silber, Laura et al *The Death of Yugoslavia* Penguin, 1996. Tie-in with the BBC series, and while it's not wholly successful without having seen the programmes, it's still a frightening blow-by-blow account of the events of the war.

Susnjar, Ante *Croatian–English/English–Croatian Dictionary and Phrasebook* Hippocrene, 2000. Good, helpful reference guide to the language.

Books

Tanner, Marcus *Croatia: A Nation Forged in War* Yale University Press, 1997. An excellent and detailed history of Croatia, by the *Independent's* correspondent during the conflict – one of the best histories currently available.

Voynovitch, Count Louis *A Historical Saunter through Dubrovnik (Ragusa)* Jadran, 1929. Nearly impossible to find, but marvellous short guide to the city from a 1929 perspective. It's amazing how little has changed in spite of both a world and a local war.

West, Rebecca *Black Lamb and Grey Falcon* Canongate Books, 1993. Without question the most comprehensive (1,200pp) and best-written account of Yugoslavia in the 1930s. Rebecca West travelled widely in Croatia (and the other republics of the former Yugoslavia) in 1936 and 1937, and spent five years researching and writing this book. Fatally flawed in places, and naïve in its conclusion, it's nonetheless by turns funny, passionate and tragic – and always brilliantly opinionated. If you come across the original two-volume hardback from the 1940s, go for it; there are excellent black-and-white photographs.

WEB RESOURCES

As you'd expect there's a mountain of information and a wealth of resources about both Dubrovnik and Croatia on the web. Here are just a handful of useful links:

Dubrovnik

web.tzdubrovnik.hr The official website of the Dubrovnik Tourist Board. Busy, but somehow less useful than it might be.

www.airport-dubrovnik.hr Official website for Čilipi airport; usefully includes live flight arrivals and departures.

www.dalmacija.net Dalmatia's own tourist information site, with online hotel bookings etc.

www.dubrovnik.hr City of Dubrovnik website. At the time of writing the English pages weren't working, unfortunately.

www.dubrovnik-online.com Unofficial site with heaps of useful and interesting information.

General

www.meteo.hr (and mirror site at **www.tel:.hr/dhmz**) Croatian Meteorological Service. Click on the flag for English and find out everything you ever wanted to know about Croatia's weather, including forecasts.

www.croatia.hr The National Tourist Board's website, with a huge amount of practical and background information.

www.hr The so-called 'Croatian Homepage', an English-language site featuring 7,500 links in hundreds of categories, all about Croatia.

www.htnet.hr/imenik Croatia's online phone directory (including an English-language option). Just what you need when it turns out the phone number listed in this guide has already changed.

www.visit-croatia.co.uk Excellent UK-based website which plugs all things Croatian and has lots of useful links (as well as an interview with this author, along with some of his Croatian pictures).

Web resources

Transport

www.adriatica.it; www.jadrolinija.hr; www.sem-marina.hr The three main ferry companies plying the Adriatic.

www.hak.hr Hrvatski Autoklub (Croatian Automobile Club). In Croatian only, though it does have an interactive traffic-snarl-up area in English.

www.ina.hr The state-owned oil company. Complete with fuel prices and the locations and opening hours of every petrol station in the country.

Government, media, etc

www.dzs.hr Croatian Bureau of Statistics. Everything you ever wanted to know.

www.hic.hr/english/index.htm Another news portal (also available in Croatian and Spanish).

www.hinet.hr Excellent customisable portal in Croatian and English, with daily news bulletins, weather, traffic, entertainment, etc.

www.hrt.hr Croatian national TV and radio (in Croatian).

www.mint.hr Ministry of Tourism. More statistics and all the forms you'll need if you're planning on starting a business in the Croatian tourist industry.

www.mvp.hr Ministry of Foreign Affairs. Everything you need to know about visa requirements etc.

WIN £100 CASH!

READER QUESTIONNAIRE

Win a cash prize of £100 for the first completed questionnaire drawn after December 31 2005.
All respondents may order a Bradt guide at half the UK retail price – please complete the order form overleaf.

Have you used any other Bradt guides? If so, which titles? . . . .
. . . .
. . . .
What other publishers' travel guides do you use regularly? . . . .
. . . .
. . . .
Where did you buy this guidebook?. . . . .
What was the main purpose of your trip to Dubrovnik (or for what other reason did you read our guide)? eg: holiday/business/charity etc. . . . .
. . . .

What other destinations would you like to see covered by a Bradt guide?

. . . .

Would you like to receive our catalogue/newsletters?

YES / NO (If yes, please complete details on opposite page)

If yes – by post or email?. . . . .

Age (circle relevant category) 16–25   26–45   46–60   60+

Male/Female (delete as appropriate)

Home country . . . .

Please send us any comments about our guide to Dubrovnik or other Bradt Travel Guides. . . . .

. . . .

. . . .

. . . .

Bradt Travel Guides
19 High Street, Chalfont St Peter, Bucks SL9 9QE, UK
Telephone: +44 (0)1753 893444 Fax: +44 (0)1753 892333
Email: info@bradtguides.com
www.bradtguides.com

CLAIM YOUR HALF-PRICE BRADT GUIDE!

To order your half-price copy of a Bradt guide, and to enter our £100 prize draw, fill in the form below, complete the questionnaire on pages 235–6, and send it to us by post, fax or email. Post and packing is free to UK addresses. A list of other city guides can be found on the inside cover; the full range of titles and prices is on our website (www.bradtguides.com).

Title	Retail price	Half price
. . . .	. . . .	. . . .
Post & packing outside UK (£2/book Europe; £3/book rest of world)		. . . .
	Total	. . . .

Name. . . . .

. . . .

Address . . . .

. . . .

Tel. . . . .   Email . . . .

❑ I enclose a cheque for £ . . . . made payable to Bradt Travel Guides Ltd
❑ I would like to pay by VISA or MasterCard
      Number. . . . .   Expiry date . . . .
❑ Please add my name to your catalogue mailing list.

BRADT TRAVEL GUIDES

Africa by Road	£13.95		*Cork City Guide*	£6.95
Albania	£13.95		*Croatia*	£12.95
Amazon	£14.95		*Dubrovnik City Guide*	£6.95
Antarctica: A Guide to the Wildlife	£14.95		*East & Southern Africa:*	
The Arctic: A Guide to Coastal			*Backpacker's Manual*	£14.95
Wildlife	£14.95		*Eccentric America*	£13.95
Armenia with Nagorno Karabagh	£13.95		*Eccentric Britain*	£11.95
Azores	£12.95		*Eccentric Edinburgh*	£5.95
Baghdad City Guide	£9.95		*Eccentric France*	£12.95
Baltic Capitals: Tallinn, Riga,			*Eccentric London*	£12.95
Vilnius, Kaliningrad	£11.95		*Eccentric Oxford*	£5.95
Bosnia & Herzegovina	£13.95		*Ecuador, Peru & Bolivia:*	
Botswana: Okavango Delta,			*Backpacker's Manual*	£13.95
Chobe, Northern Kalahari	£14.95		*Ecuador: Climbing & Hiking*	£13.95
British Isles: Wildlife of Coastal Waters	£14.95		*Eritrea*	£12.95
Budapest City Guide	£7.95		*Estonia*	£12.95
Cambodia	£11.95		*Ethiopia*	£13.95
Cameroon	£13.95		*Falkland Islands*	£13.95
Canada: North – Yukon,			*Faroe Islands*	£13.95
Northwest Territories	£13.95		*Gabon, São Tomé & Príncipe*	£13.95
Canary Islands	£13.95		*Galápagos Wildlife*	£14.95
Cape Verde Islands	£12.95		*Gambia, The*	£12.95
Cayman Islands	£12.95		*Georgia with Armenia*	£13.95
Chile	£16.95		*Ghana*	£13.95
Chile & Argentina: Trekking Guide	£12.95		*Iran*	£12.95
China: Yunnan Province	£13.95		*Iraq*	£14.95

Kabul Mini Guide	£9.95	*Riga City Guide*	£6.95
Kenya	£14.95	*River Thames: In the*	
Kiev City Guide	£7.95	*Footsteps of the Famous*	£10.95
Latvia	£12.95	*Rwanda*	£13.95
Lille City Guide	£5.95	*St Helena, Ascension, Tristan da Cunha*	£14.95
Lithuania	£12.95	*Serbia*	£13.95
Ljubljana City Guide	£6.95	*Seychelles*	£12.95
London: In the Footsteps of the Famous	£10.95	*Singapore*	£11.95
Macedonia	£13.95	*Slovenia*	£13.95
Madagascar	£14.95	*South Africa: Budget Travel Guide*	£11.95
Madagascar Wildlife	£14.95	*Southern African Wildlife*	£18.95
Malawi	£12.95	*Sri Lanka*	£12.95
Maldives	£12.95	*Sudan*	£13.95
Mali	£13.95	*Svalbard*	£13.95
Mauritius	£12.95	*Switzerland: Rail, Road, Lake*	£12.95
Mongolia	£14.95	*Tallinn City Guide*	£6.95
Montenegro	£12.95	*Tanzania*	£14.95
Mozambique	£12.95	*Tasmania*	£12.95
Namibia	£14.95	*Tibet*	£12.95
Nigeria	£14.95	*Uganda*	£13.95
North Cyprus	£12.95	*Ukraine*	£14.95
North Korea	£13.95	*USA by Rail*	£12.95
Palestine with Jerusalem	£12.95	*Venezuela*	£14.95
Panama	£13.95	*Your Child Abroad: A Travel*	
Paris, Lille & Brussels: Eurostar Cities	£11.95	*Health Guide*	£9.95
Peru & Bolivia: Backpacking &		*Zambia*	£15.95
Trekking	£12.95	*Zanzibar*	£12.95

Pocket an expert!
More city guides from Bradt

Comprehensive coverage of a range of European cities, complemented by full-colour street maps.

Budapest Adrian Phillips & Jo Scotchmer
This guide offers a fascinating insight into one of the world's great romantic capitals. A wide range of options are covered – including the caves and Roman ruins of Buda, the vibrant shops and restaurants of Pest, and the city's best walks and thermal spas.

Riga Stephen Baister & Chris Patrick
The Latvian capital is rapidly increasing in popularity as travellers tour the new map of Europe. Features in this guide include a list of the best cafés, restaurants and bars, as well as a city walking tour to allow the visitor to explore Riga's rich history and culture.

Tallinn Neil Taylor

Take a walking tour through the cobbled streets of Old Tallinn with Estonia expert, Neil Taylor. With details of local excursions and cosmopolitan bars, cafés and restaurants this is the essential guide to Estonia's beautiful medieval capital.

Ljubljana Robin & Jenny McKelvie

Slovenia's capital blends Austro-Hungarian and Italian influences, possessing both a lively nightlife buzz and classical attractions like art galleries, museums, classical music and opera. Travellers are provided with listings on a range of accommodation types, from new five-star luxury to family-run guesthouses that retain their typical Slovenian charm.

Available from all good bookshops, or by post, fax, phone or internet direct from:

Bradt Travel Guides Ltd

Tel: +44 (0)1753 893444 www.bradtguides.com

Index

Old Town (PL)

Insert Statue of St Blaise above the Ploče Gate (PL)

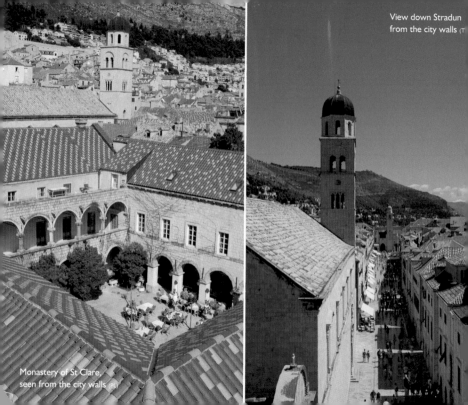

View down Stradun from the city walls (T)

Monastery of St Clare, seen from the city walls (PL)

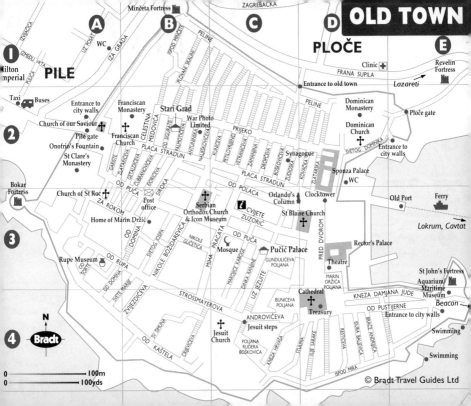

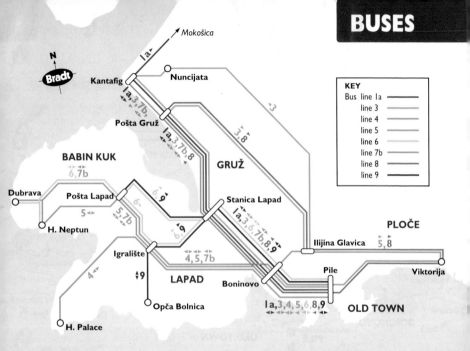